Darren Ware was born in Enfield, North London in 1971 and was educated at St George's Roman Catholic Primary School and St Ignatius College. He left home at the age of 16 and joined the army, where he served with the 2nd Battalion The Royal Green Jackets for ten years, almost three years of which was served in Northern Ireland, where he was awarded a Mention in Despatches for distinguished service. Darren also served on operations in Cyprus and Bosnia. He conducted various training exercises worldwide and was an instructor of Infantry weapons and tactics, a Gunnery Instructor and Nuclear Biological and Chemical Warfare instructor for seven and a half years, and also trained recruits for two and a half years in 1993.

He left the army in 1997 as a Corporal, after a successful career, and joined the police service. He now serves on the Armed Response Unit full time and is a reserve helicopter observer on the Air Support Unit. He has three children and lives in the North-West of England.

Dearest Brother

I still have all those happy thoughts
And dreams we had to share,
The thoughts that seem so empty now
As you're no longer there.

The bond we had was broken
When the final parting came,
As without you here beside me
Life just doesn't seem the same.

I pray each day, there'll come a time
When all my tears have dried,
I'll see you in the sunshine
And feel you at my side.

FOR THOSE WHO FIGHT FOR IT, FREEDOM
HAS A TASTE THAT THE PROTECTED WILL NEVER KNOW
'NULLI SECUNDUS'

THIS BOOK IS DEDICATED TO THE LIVES OF HER MAJESTY'S ARMED
FORCES AND CIVILIANS WHO MADE THE ULTIMATE SACRIFICE IN
THE CAUSE FOR PEACE IN NORTHERN IRELAND DURING OPERATION
BANNER FROM 14TH AUGUST 1969 – 31ST JULY 2007.

A RENDEZVOUS WITH THE ENEMY

My brother's life and death with the Coldstream Guards in Northern Ireland

Darren Ware

Helion & Company Ltd

Helion & Company Limited
26 Willow Road
Solihull
West Midlands
B91 1UE
England
Tel. 0121 705 3393
Fax 0121 711 4075
Email: info@helion.co.uk
Website: www.helion.co.uk

Published by Helion & Company 2010

Designed and typeset by Farr out Publications, Wokingham, Berkshire
Cover designed by Farr out Publications, Wokingham, Berkshire
Printed by Henry Ling Ltd, Dorchester, Dorset

Text and photographs © Darren Ware 2010

ISBN 978-1-906033-57-6

British Library Cataloguing-in-Publication Data.
A catalogue record for this book is available from the British Library.

For details of other military history titles published by Helion & Company Limited contact the above address, or visit our website: http://www.helion.co.uk.

We always welcome receiving book proposals from prospective authors.

Contents

Foreword

Our attention is now firmly focused on the outstanding work being undertaken by our troops in Afghanistan. The Northern Ireland Campaign seems to be a distant memory. This book however takes us back and provides a vivid insight through the eyes of serving soldiers who had to deal with the complexities of countering terrorism in our own country.

I recently visited the Province on business and marvelled at the changes; it is now a vibrant, modern and forward-looking country. One can only pray that the dissident groups are never in a position to take the country back to those dark days again.

Without the bravery of men like Simon Ware who sadly lost his life serving in support of the civil powers, this transition to peace could never have been achievable. There is a marvellous description of Simon by one of his colleagues describing him as being small in height (for a Guardsman!) but having the stature of twice the man with a grin from ear to ear. That will always be my memory of him patrolling across the fields of South Armagh with his GPMG at the ready.

He truly lived up to the Coldstream motto – *Nulli Secundus*.

Former Officer Commanding
Number 4 (Operations) Company
2nd Battalion Coldstream Guards
July 2010

Acknowledgements

Writing any book is not an easy achievement alone without the help from other people, no matter how big or small their assistance was. I wish to take this opportunity to thank many people for their help, encouragement and support and the many friends and colleagues who knew Simon but had no contribution to the book save for their support and encouragement in this project and during Simon's life.

I would like to thank many individuals who know who they are and whose names have been masked at their request. Andy J, for your control, contribution, morale support and encouragement; Lee Onslow, for your contribution, your telephone conversation with stories and your interest; Anthony B, for your contribution, advice and guidance over sensitive issues and your overall command; 'Moose' and 'Billy' whose details shall remain nameless, for your help at the scene of the explosion during my revisit and for your research into the photos you gave which puts the reader at the scene; OC A Company and my Company Sergeant Major 1RGJ for your contribution and welfare issues that gave me the time to sort things out at home - I have much respect for you both; Rob M, John A and Micky L, for your help and contribution; 'Johno', for your contribution, the comments you recalled and your time and hospitality for my visit to Ebrington Barracks; The Recce Platoon section commander, for your contribution and honesty with the letter - you confirmed my suspicions over one or two things, thanks for your courage and help; Sam Gibson, for your contribution and cheerful comments of Simon; Bri Dart, for your contribution, help and for the drinks in the Sergeants Mess that night on my revisit to Ebrington Barracks and Bessbrook Mill; Guy M, for your positive and powerful words addressed to the Ops Company that night to break the news; Chris P, once Simon's platoon sergeant, for your contribution and good stories; Chris C (OC Ops Company), for your contribution and support you gave my mother when you broke the news; Paul Billet, for your help at Regimental Headquarters filling in some gaps and more importantly assisting me in making contact with all those who served with Simon on the tour, and for your support back home.

I am most grateful also for the use of the two Coldstream Guards websites, www.coldstreamguards.co.uk and www.shinycapstar.com from which many comments have been received and which allowed me to catch up with Simon's muckers.

Also, a huge thank you to Duncan Rogers of Helion and Company, without whose trust this book would not have made it to print. Many thanks to all the people who did not directly contribute with its content but who have given me the encouragement to complete the project. For those who did not wish to contribute or reply, I understand that you have done so for your personal reasons and only hope that your thoughts are positive and that you have each dealt with things in your own way. A thank you to all the readers who have shown interest in reading this personal impact story of what happened to my brother and our family as a result of operations in Northern Ireland, a story that is echoed so many, many times. And finally, a thank you to all those servicemen, women and civilian personnel who, for more than 38 years, put their lives at risk daily and put their heart and effort to working towards a lasting peace in the fight against terrorism. For those who did not return we thank you for your sacrifice.

Abbreviations

2i/c	Second-in-Command of a unit. Could be of a section, company or battalion
ATO	Ammunition Technician Officer (army bomb disposal)
ARF	Airborne Reaction Force. A unit of soldiers on standby to react to a terrorist incident.
AWOL	Absent With Out Leave
APC	Armoured Personnel Carrier
Bergen	A large back pack used to carry larger and heavier items of equipment
Bn, Battalion	A unit of about 650 infantry soldiers. Each regiment may have 2 or 3 battalions e.g. 1st Bn Royal Green Jackets (1RGJ)
CCTV	Closed Circuit Television
CSM	Company Sergeant Major. In charged of admin and discipline of a Company of soldiers amounting to about 120 soldiers
Chinook	Twinned rotor large heavy-duty helicopter capable of carrying a large number of soldiers
Contact Point	A point where the army or police patrol came under attack
Command Wire	Twinflex electrical wire attached to the IED and the other end attached to a firing pack.
CO	Commanding Officer of a battalion of about 650 soldiers
Firing Pack	Attached to the command wire which controls the initiation of the IED
Firing Point	A point at which the terrorists would mount their attack
GPMG	General Purpose Machine Gun, known as a 'Jimpy'
Heli Pad	Helicopter landing site
HME	Home Made Explosive. Usually Ammonium Nitrate Sugar (ANS)
IED	Improvised Explosive Device
ICP	Incident Control Point
IAAG	Improvised Anti-Armour Grenade. A home made grenade sometimes fixed to a pole with fins to aid stability in flight, which would be thrown against Land Rovers and other armoured vehicles.
Killing Zone	The area of the contact point where casualties could be taken
Lynx	Type of helicopter capable of carrying about 6-8 people
MK15	Mark 15 'coffee jar' improvised hand grenade used by the IRA
NAAFI	Navy Army and Air Force Institute. A welfare club providing amusement, entertainment, social and shopping facilities worldwide.
NCO	Non Commissioned Officer i.e. Corporal, Sergeant etc
NIPIN	Northern Ireland Personal Identification Number
NISR	Northern Ireland Search Record
'NIG'	New Intake Group. Green Jacket slang for a new recruit joining the battalion.
OC	Officer Commanding a company of about 120 soldiers

UDR	Ulster Defence Regiment
PSNI	Police Service of Northern Ireland (previously known as the RUC)
PVCP	Permanent Vehicle Check Point. Large permanent structure built at strategic locations to check and monitor traffic to and from the border.
QRF	Quick Reaction Force (similar to ARF but use vehicles)
RUC	Royal Ulster Constabulary (now known as the Police Service of Northern Ireland)
RSM	Regimental Sergeant Major. In charge of the admin and discipline of a battalion amounting to about 650 soldiers
R&R	Rest and Recuperation. A short period of time away from operations on leave
RMO	Regimental Medical Officer
RESA	Royal Engineers Search Advisor
REST	Royal Engineers Search Team
Scrap yard confetti	A collection of nuts and bolts placed inside an IED to have the effect of shrapnel.
SCBC	Section Commanders Battle Course
Sitrep	Situation Report
SASC	Small Arms School Corps
SAS	Special Air Service
SF Base	Security Forces Base. Could be a small, medium or large fixed base from which troops operate from.
SOCO	Scenes of Crimes Officer (Forensic examiner)
Semtex	A powerful explosive
'Sweat'	A soldier who had been in service longer than you, with more experience.
Top Cover	The term used when a helicopter gives aerial support to another helicopter or ground troops
TAOR	Tactical Area of Operational Responsibility. Usually referred to as area of responsibility
UFO	Unit Families Officer
Webbing	A collection of pouches secured on a belt and worn around waist to carry items of equipment and ammunition.
Wessex	Type of helicopter capable of carrying about 12 people
WIS	Weapons Intelligence Section

Preface

Some three years ago, whilst writing my first book on the Northern Ireland troubles, I had cause to meet Darren who was immensely helpful with my research. Indeed, he not only appeared in my first book on the troubles, *A Long Long War* but more importantly, he became my friend.

We had both served in the finest Regiment in the British Army – the Royal Green Jackets – albeit, many years apart, so we had much in common. I was delighted that he chose to write about his brother Simon who was sadly killed in Carrickovaddy Woods, close to Crossmaglen and in Darren's own time in Northern Ireland.

Then he asked me to write the preface to his long-awaited book and I accepted the honour with great alacrity – it is an absolute pleasure and a privilege to do so.

I know that Darren was very close to his brother and his loss was a tragedy to the Ware family and to his grieving widow Carol, and he rightly regards him as a hero. To those who served in Ulster we knew the fears and the dangers but we also shared the camaraderie and the love of our platoon comrades, and they are men who we will never forget.

Darren's excellent book describes Simon's time in 'Bandit country' and his eventual death caused by a massive IRA landmine whilst on a rural patrol. He also looks at his own time in Northern Ireland where he was ultimately awarded a coveted Mention in Dispatches for saving the lives of his patrol comrades after foiling an IRA booby trapped device in a derelict house.

I commend this well written, moving and honest account of what it was like for a squaddie serving in the streets and country lanes of Northern Ireland.

If you want the truth about what happened during a forgotten war on our own doorsteps, I strongly recommend that you read this excellent account of Darren Ware's brother Simon who tragically became one of 1,294 British soldiers who died in or as a direct consequence of the troubles.

Darren; thanks for the honour of writing this preface. I am both moved and humbled.

Ken M Wharton, Queensland, Australia, July 2010
Author of *A Long Long War*, *Bullets, Bombs and Cups of Tea* and *Bloody Belfast*

Introduction

M any books have been written about the 'Troubles' in Northern Ireland describing its history from 1969 to the time of the end of military involvement and the conclusion of Operation Banner in July 2007. There seems to be a lot of history written since the early 70's until the early to mid 1990's, but much more of the 90's was not reported, as it seemed that the conflict was reducing in violence and heading towards an end. The Civil Rights marches that took place in Northern Ireland in 1969 were the turning point of the deployment of British troops and in the early part of that year troops were deployed to protect the vital installations that remained a terrorist threat. By the middle of August the rioting increased, which led to the deployment of British troops on the streets of Northern Ireland. It was a decision and a time in current history that would affect many people and most importantly the population of Northern Ireland - the people who wanted the change and the people who didn't; for those who didn't want the military intrusion it would affect their lives, their livelihoods and at times their thoughts and opinions, which would fluctuate over the years and bring devastation to their lives.

Late afternoon on 14th August 1969 the 1st Battalion The Prince Of Wales' Own Regiment marched into Londonderry to assist the Royal Ulster Constabulary in the defeat of terrorism and to assist in public disorder. For the soldiers who marched into the city that day, it was an unfamiliar environment and an unfamiliar campaign that would change and become unpredictable. Those soldiers had left their hometowns to enter someone else's hometown with its unfamiliar surroundings and unsure people. For the occupants of Londonderry, the soldiers who marched onto their streets and doorsteps were unfamiliar, they too did not know what to expect from this army which was sent into their hometown by Britain's Government.

The following day troops deployed onto the streets of Belfast and it was clear by this stage that the British Government had committed themselves to another sensitive situation that needed to be resolved and just like the soldiers of the First World War, they were told that they would be home and out of Northern Ireland by Christmas. This was a misunderstanding that was gladly met by the soldiers, but those living in Northern Ireland who felt that protection was needed were led to believe that it was only temporary. This was a protection that the RUC and others who were vulnerable felt needed to be maintained. Initially the troops received a positive welcome from the Catholic community but as the years went by and following the tragic events of Bloody Sunday on 30th January 1972, that situation changed.

In February 1971 the IRA killed its first British soldier in the conflict; Gunner Robert Curtis was 20 years old when he was shot dead in a fierce firefight in the New Lodge area of Belfast. This was an incident which also claimed the life of another colleague. In February 1997, six days short of 26 years later, the Provisional IRA killed its last soldier in the current conflict. Lance Bombardier Stephen Restorick was shot dead as he manned a vehicle checkpoint at the security force base at Bessbrook in South Armagh. Could Stephen Restorick's and countless others murders been prevented? The author believes so.

In March of 1991 new peace talks began between Sinn Fein, the IRA and the British government in an attempt to resolve the then current peace talks. As a serving soldier in County Tyrone at the time I was informed that the talks were estimated to take 10 weeks, but more than 10 years later the situation remained completely unsolved. A frustrating situation for many, but it is one that would never have been resolved overnight.

Shortly before 31st August 1994 the IRA announced that they would begin a ceasefire, or rather what they described as a 'cessation of hostilities' as from midnight. At the time I was traveling in an army 4-tonne truck across Otterburn training area in Northumberland when I read the front-page headlines and my complete attention was drawn to this historic news. I was surprised at the announcement but I was in two minds. Firstly I thought it would be good to end the violence for a lasting peace and to prevent further loss of life, but on the other hand I felt that the loss of lives through those years would have been a waste and that all may be forgotten. However in February 1996 this ceasefire came to an end with a massive bomb attack in London's Dockland area which claimed the lives of two newsagents working close to Canary Wharf. Again, the Provisional IRA declared another ceasefire almost 18 months later in July 1997, which to this day remains in force.

The Good Friday Agreement of April 1998 which led to the early release of terrorist prisoners in September of the same year was a further step in the Peace process. Clearly this was a victorious event in the eyes of the convicted terrorists and their families and supporters. Some of these prisoners had only been sentenced in recent years having received life sentences, multiple life sentences and other custodial sentences for their involvement in the murders of soldiers, police officers and civilians. They had been released early, allowed to continue with their lives and many of them were hailed as heroes, 'heroes' of a political war. For those relatives and friends of the soldiers, police officers and civilians who had been killed, the early release was a bitter blow and created a huge sense of injustice and insult. In the late 90's and early 2000's Northern Ireland had remained in the background of military history and home affairs and had been taken over by more recent hostilities such as Gulf War 2, Sierra Leone and Afghanistan.

There came a day in September 1998 when the distinctive tall observation towers close to the border of South Armagh and other security installations began to be dismantled. For years they had been the eyes and ears of the army and police assisting in the build-up of intelligence and the protection of the area against terrorist attacks. It was an historic event which people thought would never occur, as the eyes and ears of military operations were reduced. Similarly, there was a reduction in military presence when on Thursday 11th August 2003 the last army patrol of Londonderry took place and the following day a national newspaper reported the headlines - 'Last patrol on the streets of fear'. The 1st Battalion Green Howards ended joint army and police patrols in Londonderry and handed over Ebrington Barracks to the police after years of a bittersweet military presence.

The 31st July 2007 saw the official end to Operation Banner, the British Army's deployment to Northern Ireland. The build-up to this date saw many observation towers being dismantled, permanent vehicle checkpoints being removed and security force bases being handed back over to local authorities. There were mixed feelings from the hundreds of thousands of people who had been affected by 'The Troubles'. This was a time of huge change and a time to move on for a better future. There was no fanfare as soldiers left the security force bases for the last time and in particularly Bessbrook Mill, which had been the busiest heli ort in Europe for the duration of Operation Banner. There was no extravaganza or parades as the soldiers left and it seemed a case of 'last one out turn the lights off and shut the door'.

Over the 38 years of operations in Northern Ireland 300,000 soldiers had deployed on routine patrols in the province in both urban and rural environments. In the early 70's tactics were developed until it was realised that it had come to a fight against terrorists, and that the British army were staying to assist the RUC in the defeat of them. Military intelligence gained information on the terrorist organisations, which enabled troops to direct their tactics towards a certain threat. Thousands of routine patrols deployed throughout the six counties over many years of covert and overt operations, one in particular was no different.

On 11th March 1991 the 2nd Battalion Coldstream Guards deployed to Northern Ireland to begin a six-month tour of South Armagh, operating in 'Bandit Country'. This book is about one patrol, one soldier and one story. Corporal Simon Ware was a member of call sign Yankee One Zero Bravo who deployed from their base in Bessbrook Mill, South Armagh on a routine three-day patrol in the Newtownhamilton area close to the border on 15th August 1991. At 22 years old this was his second tour of the Northern Ireland. By the third day the patrol had completed all their tasks and were moving north through a wooded area towards their helicopter pick-up point north of Carrickovaddy Wood. Twenty minutes before the helicopter was due to land a huge explosion tore up the ground tragically killing Corporal Simon Ware.

This story introduces Simon's life, sets the scene of the tour, the patrol and the subsequent events. It is written from the heart of Simon's brother, Darren, and those involved; it is honest and to the point, and in graphic detail.

Readers of this book should understand that the author has conducted years of enquiries and investigation into the research of the circumstances aided by many agencies. Due to the sensitivity of military operations in South Armagh and Northern Ireland certain aspects are in brief detail. The surnames of all involved have been omitted in order to respect their privacy and security although all of the Christian names remain the same in order to set the scene. Where appointments have been used, it is for those who were in that position in 1991 and has been done so to preserve privacy. Individuals who have contributed information and help have recalled events from that day. Those who were members of the patrol and those who were at the scene immediately afterwards to view the scene and deal with the aftermath have memories and feelings in their minds forever - those memories that were bloodied and that have scarred their minds.

My thoughts are with those people who on this occasion, and many other occasions, have been forced to face the aftermath of violent death in the fight for peace; those people that have had no choice but to witness close friends killed by acts of terrorism, and whose memories and mental scars will never fade.

1

Hard times, terrorists and bombs

I led the patrol of eight soldiers on a routine foot patrol as I exited the rear of Strabane RUC station just after 11pm on Friday April 3rd 1992. I infiltrated the northern part of the town using the remote rural area as my cover in an effort not to be compromised too soon. The route took me along Church Street leading downhill into the town centre to Meetinghouse Street; it was a very busy evening being a Friday. As I passed the large graveyard to my right, with its church nestled in amongst the darkened grounds and high walls, the ambient streetlights illuminated the busy Friday night town. A figure in the alleyway to my left fifteen metres in front drew my attention as he fumbled around near to parked vehicles amongst the darkened shadows. I halted the patrol and observed him for a few seconds through the SUSAT sight on top of my weapon, which afforded me an amount of magnification.

Trying to make out the identity of the figure my suspicions were confirmed when I recognised the male as a known IRA terrorist, and my actions during the night which followed were to save lives.

℘

It was Monday 16th November 1987 and I left my house in urban North London and boarded the train at Southbury Road railway station, a quiet station at Ponders End. I was 16 years old, dressed in a Burton's suit and carrying the suitcase that contained my worldly possessions that I hoped would help maintain my survival. Lonely, nervous and full of anticipation I had said goodbye to my girlfriend, Lisa, and my family, and left with a heart full of emotion and uncertainty into the real world, not knowing what to expect – the world that only months earlier my school teachers had warned me of if I was to make a break for life. Excited and determined I continued my journey. I walked the short distance to the train station which was only about half a mile away up the hill. It was a cold and overcast November morning as I walked through my hometown passing people who were going about their normal business and daily routine, passing those houses and shops that were shuttered down or boarded up with signs saying 'Closed' or 'Gone' showing failed homes and unsuccessful businesses in the 80's. My destiny would be decided by the journey ahead. My dad said goodbye to me at the platform and off I went.

Some hours later, after a thoughtful journey, I arrived at Winchester train station where I joined several other similarly-dressed civilians in the same situation as me and as I alighted the train I looked around aimlessly, wondering what my next step was. For the soldiers who greeted us, we stood out like sore thumbs and we were then shepherded by the NCO, who checked our names on the nominal roll, and instructed us firmly to stand to attention and address him as Corporal. Then, it was onto a coach for our next journey along Andover Road North, a straight Roman road out of Winchester. The coach turned left onto the short windy entrance to Sir John Moore Barracks, a magnificent brand new barracks which was the home of the Light Division, and had opened the previous year.

Standing proud and prominent next to the guardroom was the large life-size bronze statue of Sir John Moore, flanked each side by buglers of the Light Division.

This was to be my home for the next eight and a half months whilst I completed my basic training in Inkerman Platoon of the Junior Soldiers' Company. Intake day was fast and furious and no sooner had I had got off the train at Winchester my life was changed – it was not going to be easy. Although having spent some years in the army cadets, I had some limited army knowledge, I kept that advantage to myself for the time being and played the 'grey man' so as not to compromise myself. We were formed up together in three ranks and doubled everywhere to be shown around the camp. Perhaps the choice of wearing my new Burton's suit was not a practical choice in hindsight. As I stood in a silent line outside the Quartermaster's Clothing Store waiting to be issued with my kit and clothing I observed instructors shouting at other recruits, others were being beasted and a variety of various military activities going on. I daren't move my head to look around through fear of being noticed and being beasted as a consequence. Therefore my eyes were like that of an Action Man 'eagle eyes' to see what was going on. Back at the clothing store my equipment and clothing was thrown at me and as I quickly crammed it into the two green army kit bags I was issued the store man shouted out the items. I thought, what was coming next? There was no time to check the items for my own satisfaction and I was instructed to "…sign here". As we were hurriedly marched back to the accommodation our kit was thrown into our locker followed immediately by screaming instructions to form up outside to have the process repeated. " … Ware, get over here …." "Mattress, mattress cover, two sheets, three blankets, two pillows and bedding cover … Sign here" then "get outside" then we were doubled back to the block. There I was, struggling to carry it all as I quickly went back to the room. That night I sat on my bed thinking of the easy life at home that I had just left behind and wondered what was for the best. My positive thoughts kicked in then. I was only 16 years old and I convinced myself of the positive life ahead and was adamant that I was doing the right thing. I was in a room of 10 soldiers in my section and there were four other rooms in the platoon, all of us in the same boat. I persevered and pressed on.

That night we were shown how to iron our uniform, shown how to make our beds and present them in the morning. We were shown how to shower, how to shave and how to present ourselves, our locker and our equipment. The weeks and months ahead would prove hard for some as people faltered, fell by the wayside, gave in, got back-squadded or went AWOL. Training in the months ahead was easy, comfortable, horrible, enjoyable and most of the time very hard, both physically and mentally. My positive attitude of things getting better gave me the strength to push on as I didn't want to fail myself.

For the first six weeks my life was to be restricted and leaving camp within that time was not an option. Our confines of the camp was restricted to the accommodation or the NAAFI, and the once a week hobby night kept the activities varied. I first chose to do weight training but soon it wore off and I then changed it to indoor shooting but that soon wore off too, so I went back to weight training and just looked busy in the gym, until one of the training corporals who was a body builder soon got us all into a motivated workout. Since then I suppose I got used to the gym routine.

Two weeks into my training I 'phoned home to be told by my mother that my grandfather had died. I then thought that there would be a short period of release to get away for a few days for the funeral, but I was so sadly wrong. I mentioned it to my section

The Royal Green Jacket cap badge. Worn with pride throughout my career.

commander, who did not straightaway assume that I would be released to go home, and to my surprise I was refused any compassionate leave. It was at this point that I realised how hard and emotionless the army could be. They really meant it when we were told we were confined to camp for six weeks.

Pay in the army was calculated on a daily rate and you were paid every day of the year, which was great when you think that you are paid for days off on leave. In 1987 my daily rate was £9.19 before tax, and as it was my first full-time job I did not complain. Our weekly limit was £20 to draw out as cash from the pay office, which meant that spending was tight. This is all I had to purchase toiletries, stationery and phone calls and what little I had left was a luxury. Food and accommodation was already paid for.

Once into the swing of things, basic training was going well. Before I knew it I had completed the first six weeks which earned me my Royal Green Jacket beret and cap badge, plus a weekend leave pass with a bit of freedom.

On my return to camp some restrictions were lifted as we were allowed out of camp and given a bit more cash to spend. The big boost too was that a new intake had arrived and we were no longer the newest platoon of recruits and a step closer to being the 'senior' platoon. Basic training was a mixture of mostly hard, demanding and challenging activities, but looking back at each day and week it was enjoyable. The instructors treated us with discipline and punishment, meaning that if one of us messed up then we all got the punishment. It was all part of military discipline, teamwork and training and we accepted what we got, but we were pissed off with it. Once the training day was completed we got it into our heads that it was a time for relief and rest and the instructors had finished and gone home. But to our surprise there was always time for an excuse to discipline the platoon with a ritual beasting session in our own time. I recall one of many occasions when we were beasted on the parade square at the rear of our accommodation block, more often than not 'change parades' were the order of the night. The mode of dress started by being easy, then it followed by a physically hard task and then it just got worse and worse .....
"Regimental tracksuit, two minutes, go ..." Then off we sprinted into the block making sure that the whole platoon was formed up outside all dressed in tracksuit within two minutes ready for an inspection. You knew that it was going to be impossible for all 40 of us to get changed and outside within two minutes and then get inspected without any fault. And that was just their excuse to then beast us on the square with fitness training and then step it up a gear with the next mode of dress " ... Normal working dress, 2 minutes, go ..." and again off we went. As a platoon we were never going to meet our target and again we were beasted. Time and time again the dress changed until we had worn every issued piece of uniform and been beasted in it until our lockers were trashed. After an hour or two of the beasting session then we were given an impossible time scale for a room and locker inspection. And of course we failed that because our kit and lockers were trashed and we were all knackered.

Darren receives his recruit prize for Best Section Commander from General
Sir Peter de la Billière at his passing-out parade in July 1988

My time in the cadets had paid off as my section commander soon realised that I had a bit of military knowledge, which helped me progress well. Before I knew it, our training was coming to an end and the talk of our passing out parade was the topic of most conversations. We soon learned that that General Sir Peter de la Billière was to be our inspecting officer. He was an extremely high-ranking and successful officer who commanded British troops in the Gulf War of 1991. He was once in the Royal Green Jackets and was also a commander in the SAS and was a highly decorated and respected officer.

On a hot summer's day in August 1988 Inkerman Platoon stood proud outside the armoury, adjacent but out of sight of the huge drill square that was now packed with proud parents, friends and relatives. Our platoon, now a lot smaller than it was on November 16th, was brought 'ready'. The sound of the regimental band struck up and off we stepped at the regimental quick march of 140 paces to the minute along the slope and up towards the drill square to the chapel and left into the sight of the proud waiting audience. There were no verbal drill commands as all movements were executed at the sound of the base drum. On marching onto the square my heart and mouth filled with immense pride and emotion, as I had worked so hard over the last eight months and now it was all paying off. As the base drum sounded the last beat of the regimental quick march, it was the signal for the parade to come to a halt and an impressive facing right halt was executed to the erupting sound of the applauding crowd. There we stood, to rapturous applause, to the immense pride of a standing audience, our own hearts beating with pride and standing an extra six inches tall, with the drill commands screamed across the square.

A few days before the parade I was informed that I was one of the prize winners and for my efforts during basic training I was awarded the prize for the Best Recruit Section Commander. Along with other prize winners I took centre stage on the drill square to receive my award from General de la Billière along with a handshake. A treasured moment.

Following the pass-out parade I left Sir John Moore Barracks and joined the Second Battalion The Royal Green Jackets and was posted to Battlesbury Barracks at Warminster, undertaking the role of Infantry Trials and Development Unit. Others left to join other battalions to be posted to various postings such as Northern Ireland, Germany and Gibraltar. Two weeks leave preceded that, whereby I enjoyed a well-earned relaxing time and celebrated the end of my training and the start of a successful and enjoyable career. But the reality and dangers of army life were highlighted when only a few days into my leave I learned the news of the Ballygawley bus bombing in Omagh, Northern Ireland. The IRA had attacked a bus full of Light Infantry soldiers returning from leave to Lisanelly Barracks, Omagh. One of the soldiers who I passed out with on the drill square that day was killed in that attack – his life cut short in his prime, he had not reached his first posting.

Life in battalion was now a lot different and it was a case of fending for yourself – if you were not in the right place at the right time with the correct kit then you were in the shit. I managed and settled in quite well in 15 Platoon D Company.

The posting to Warminster was only for four months as I had joined the regiment at the end of a two and a half year posting there, and the next posting was just across the Home Counties to Connaught Barracks in Dover. The role there was now that of mechanised infantry, and would consist of several exercises both in the UK and overseas and an operational tour of Northern Ireland.

The reality of an enjoyable career began with the annual inter-company competition, whereby clues were located in places where you had to be adventurous to find them as part of a team. The one that was found before my task involved soldier's abseiling down the white cliffs of Dover to hunt it out. It was successfully found, which left me and two others tasked with the next clue to solve. At 0500hrs we were summoned to the Company Sergeant Major's office to be given a ferry ticket to go to France to hunt it out – oh what a hard task that would be! We were instructed to find the answer and return on the next boat – yeah right! Using our initiative we decided to have a few beers on the crossing and once in Calais it did not take us long to find the clue and again using collective initiative we telephoned the answer back and consumed more beer on the ferry back to Dover. Needless to say we were not required to find any more clues.

Germany was our next exercise for a month or so, which was not greatly exciting but afforded six weeks away immersed in the consumption of quality German beer and social life. During this exercise we conducted some adventure training in a scenic region of Moenchengladbach, whereby amongst other things, canoeing was the activity of the day. I had never done any watersports before so we were all lectured on the dos and don'ts, water safety and rescue techniques. So when you capsized in the canoe you would expect the nearby canoeists to help in your recovery. Like fuck though!! – I capsized and it felt like a lifetime before anyone righted my canoe. Once I had surfaced I learned that it was one of the instructors that had intervened to right my canoe and saved me. So it was from that day onwards, when I thought I was about to drown, that I lost all interest in the sport.

It was not long before the battalion then embarked on training for Northern Ireland, and at the beginning of 1989 the regiment then deployed to County Fermanagh and took up company and platoon locations on the border region in February. In the four month tour our platoon was to rotate around the three towns of Newtownbutler, Rosslea and Lisnaskea, manning three border permanent vehicle checkpoints. I was very apprehensive as it was my first operational tour of Northern Ireland and I was only 18. During our training we were made aware of recent terrorist attacks on all of the three locations that we were deploying to, but fortunately the tour was quiet, as at the time the Fermanagh Brigade of PIRA was not too active and had temporarily disbanded. However on our return to the UK, our places having been taken over by the Scots Guards, we were to hear that two of the vehicle checkpoints that we had manned had come under serious attacks by the IRA, resulting in the loss of lives.

In June 1990 we were treated to another overseas six week exercise in Canada. I had now settled in very well to battalion life and was working hard and earning success and respect. The exercise consisted of four weeks in Wainwright on training and live firing, the hardest of which was to fend off the mosquitoes and bearing up to the heat. The exercise culminated in a Battalion-size deliberate attack on a large enemy position, and as the attack warning order filtered down to the platoon I was ushered away to a destination unknown. Before long I had been driven to Battalion HQ in a secure rural area and met by the commanding officer. I could not believe what I was now being told – "Rifleman Ware, you are now the Commanding Officer, you must take the enemy position by 12 noon, here are your Company Commanders, this is your radio operator and you can use that helicopter for a recce of the enemy location, you have not got long."

I could not believe the position I was now in. I had a Gazelle helicopter, four Company Commanders, a Reconnaissance Platoon Commander and the whole Battalion of 600 soldiers at my command and peril. Over the past few years I was aware that I had earned respect and was looked upon as one of the better Riflemen in the platoon, but not so much that I had been recommended to command the Battalion attack on the final exercise, commanding 600 men. Along with the platoon commander of the Reconnaissance Platoon I was flown in the Gazelle helicopter on a short recce and I ordered a right flanking attack on the enemy position, which was company strength in numbers and well dug-in on a large hill. I had detailed each of the company commanders and told them to implement their plan. I then watched the five companies of the battalion, comprising about 120 in each, advance on the enemy position as I took up position in the rear and observed as I commanded 600 men in a deliberate attack. Fantastic! That was the culmination of a busy and hard-working four week exercise which was then followed by five days leave in the capital, Edmonton.

The platoon took advantage of a cheap hotel package and spent five days shopping, drinking and enjoying the biggest waterworld in Canada at the Edmonton shopping mall. The last ten days was spent adventure training in the magnificent landscape and scenery of the rocky mountains of Jasper National Park in Banff. We had several activities to indulge in but our time was flexible and on one day instead of rock climbing I had convinced half a dozen others to go trout fishing in Lake Louisiana instead. I had arranged the duty driver to drop us off and pick us up a few hours later. Once our fishing equipment was loaded then the beer was placed on board too. As the beer flowed well, some fish were caught but not with much enthusiasm. Our noise, food and rowdy behaviour was soon quietened when our secluded fishing spot was visited by a family of brown bear cubs followed closely by their large mother and even larger father bear. Apart from quite a sobering experience the incident passed when the inquisitive family moved on, and our transport soon arrived, thankfully.

Our return to Dover in August of 1990 was followed by a few weeks of hard-earned leave and on my return I completed the Junior NCO's Cadre and was promoted to Lance Corporal in October at the age of only 19. Again this was a massive transition stage as the battalion was now warned off to go back to Northern Ireland for a two and a half year tour in January 1991. This was a time when Iraq had only just invaded Kuwait in August 1990, and our posting to Northern Ireland was going to be Omagh, the place where only two years earlier the fatal Ballygawley bus bombing had occurred.

Training had begun in earnest at the end of the year and by the beginning of February 1991 plans were finalised and we went on pre-deployment leave.

On the 3rd March 1991, my 20th birthday, we deployed to Northern Ireland and on our arrival our platoon was tasked with providing escorts and the Quick Reaction Force for any incidents in the Omagh area. There was no room for settling in – by the time I had got into bed for some rest then I was roused soon after midnight to escort the ATO to a bomb explosion in the Republican border town of Strabane. Welcome back to Northern Ireland and I had only been there 12 hours! I was roused by the Guard Commander and instructed to make straight to the Battalion Ops Room, which was just across the drill square. I felt in a position of responsibility as I was only the section second-in-command. I woke one other from my section and told him to rouse the rest as I dashed across to receive my instructions.

The contact point of the bomb attack in Strabane on 3rd March 1991. The firing point was the upstairs window of the house behind the embankment.

At 10pm on the 3rd March 1991 a joint army and RUC foot patrol came under attack in the Republican Head Of Town estate in Strabane. The IED which had been concealed in a small embankment on Cemetery Road was detonated when the patrol passed. The device was a command wire IED placed by the roadside in the form of an improvised claymore mine. The command wire went into a house which had been taken over, one female was held hostage and the firing point was in the upstairs rear bedroom. The patrol escaped injury.

I was briefed by the Ops Officer that a patrol from the Royal Green Jackets who were being familiarised by a patrol from The Worcester and Sherwood Foresters had been contacted by an IED in the Head Of The Town estate in Strabane and that I was to lead the escort for the ATO team vehicles to the RV point. The Ops Officer told me: "Cpl Ware, this is the first operational battalion deployment so get it right" – I had not been in the province 12 hours, I had only been in bed two hours and I had a massive responsibility on my shoulders. With huge relief I delivered the ATO team to the RV point, to the relief of the Ops officer. The task complete, we resumed to Omagh at 0330hrs.

During the operational tour the battalion had four operational companies which were tasked with providing operations in Strabane and Castlederg border towns, operations in Omagh, guards and duties in Omagh and training and leave. The years ahead provided busy times, fun, excitement, boredom and sadness. On one incident whilst on Castlederg Ops our task was spent manning the permanent vehicle checkpoint at Clady, a very small checkpoint at a three-way junction on the road from Sion Mills where it split two ways, crossing the border only one hundred or so metres in front. It was during one of our stints there that we were subjected to a grenade attack by a Mk 15 'coffee jar' grenade that was thrown over the perimeter fence at night time, although it partially detonated and failed to explode. It had landed next to the accommodation block and the checkpoint was evacuated overnight whilst the ATO cleared the device at first light. It was a vulnerable time as we had patrolled the local area until morning and now during the hours that it took the ATO to clear the device we remained a target as we continued to patrol throughout the morning. The device was soon cleared and became one of those that were from a bad batch that continued to fail to detonate.

A similar attack took place whilst operating as part of the Strabane Ops platoon when I was coming to the end of a 12 hour daytime patrol. Our changeover routine was varied and on this occasion I and the relieving section commander had decided to change over on the ground. He had deployed with his section from the police station into the Ballycolman estate from the south and once he had entered, then I exited with my section from the northern part of the estate, a distance of about 50 meters. No sooner had I exited I heard his radio transmission that he had entered the estate, then I heard those fateful words " ….Contact, wait out…". 'Shuggy's' team had been subjected to a Mk 15 grenade attack which again had failed to detonate but had landed at the feet of one of his Riflemen, causing the glass to smash but luckily the device did not explode. Along with the QRF from Strabane police station, I had immediately re-entered the estate but with so many rat runs, escape routes and safe houses we were playing catch-up with the terrorist's escape. It was now the task of the ATO to make this device safe. Another near-miss.

By the end of 1991 I had received a warning that I was to be sent on the Section Commanders' Battle Course in January 1992, a 12-week course which qualified me for promotion to corporal. It enabled me to command and control a section of 8 soldiers, and in the absence of the platoon sergeant, then control and administer a platoon of 34 men. Although the course was not the most comfortable of ones I managed to pass it, having come top student out of 96 in Phase One, which was the weapons instruction phase.

I had been away from Northern Ireland and I was eager and determined to return and achieve our aim and continue to fight terrorism. I was aware that I would soon be posted out to the training battalion to train recruits but I wanted to achieve maximum operational experience before I left.

I led the patrol of eight soldiers on a routine foot patrol and I exited the rear of Strabane RUC station just after 11pm on Friday April 3rd 1992. I infiltrated the northern part of the town using the remote rural area as my cover in an effort not to be compromised too soon. The route took me along Church Street leading downhill into the town centre to Meetinghouse Street – it was a very busy evening, being a Friday. As I passed the large graveyard to my right, with its church nestled in amongst the darkened grounds and high walls, the ambient streetlights illuminated the busy Friday night town. A figure in the alleyway to my left fifteen metres in front drew my attention as he fumbled around near to parked vehicles amongst the darkened shadows. I halted the patrol and observed him for a few seconds through the SUSAT sight on top of my weapon, which afforded me an amount of magnification.

My suspicions were confirmed when I recognised the male as a known IRA terrorist. At the same time, but unaware to me, the owner of a boarded-up shop on Main Street had reported suspicious activity to the police. I then instructed my 2 i/c and his team to lay in wait in the graveyard whilst I waited nearby to develop my plan of action. I had contacted the ops room and instructed them to deploy the QRF to the main gates of the police station and instructed my 2 i/c to observe and challenge the male should he move off. My 2i/c informed me that the suspect had moved off and I instructed him to follow and stop and search him. He was soon stopped and searched on Meetinghouse Street and found with nothing of any interest on him. I joined the patrol and confirmed that the male I had earlier observed through the sight of my weapon was this male. I could not believe my luck but was disappointed that nothing was found. Pursuing my suspicion, I returned to the same alleyway to conduct a discreet search during which I found a CB radio secreted in the corner of a wall. Convinced that the same male would return, and determined to pursue my suspicion, I instructed my 2i/c to redeploy to the graveyard to observe the alleyway whilst I briefed the platoon sergeant and QRF at the police station gates, only a few yards away. During this quick brief my 2i/c informed me that the same male had returned and picked something up which was later identified as the same CB radio I had earlier located in the alleyway. My instructions were to detain him for police arrival, which was done. When the police arrived their reaction was jubilant and described the situation as "could not have happened to a nicer guy!!!" The suspect, having been arrested for conspiracy to cause an explosion and to murder members of the security forces, was conveyed to Strand Road RUC Station at Londonderry where his detention was authorised.

Having analysed the suspicious activity earlier reported and the suspicious incident I had just dealt with I consulted my street map of Strabane. My attention was drawn to the area of Church Street and Meetinghouse Street and I noticed on the ground that Church Street featured a boarded-up shop premises that afforded a clear view from the alleyway further up Church Street where the arrested male had been disturbed. I suggested that

By the QUEEN'S Order the name of
Lance Corporal (Acting Corporal)
Darren Roderick Warren Ware,
The Royal Green Jackets
was published in the London Gazette on
12 October 1993,
as mentioned in a Despatch for distinguished service.
I am charged to record
Her Majesty's high appreciation.

Secretary of State for Defence

Darren's Mention In Despatches for Distinguished service
in Northern Ireland. A treasured award.

the area be put locally out of use by police and army patrols that night and that a search be conducted at first light. This was duly done and shortly before midday on Saturday 4th April a bomb was located behind the boarded-up shop at 61 Main Street, consisting of 14lb of HME in a paint tin connected to a firing pack. The device was attached to a command wire laid ready to detonate. Also found at the scene was a compatible CB radio of exactly the same model found in the alleyway where the arrested male was detained and both CB radios were tuned to the same channel and switched on. ATO was tasked to clear the device and confirmed that the bomb was ready to detonate. For my actions and command and control that dark distant night I was to be awarded a Mention in Despatches. My citation reads:

> By the Queen's Order, the name of LCpl (Acting Cpl) Darren Ware, The Royal Green Jackets, was published in the London Gazette on 12 October 1993 as Mentioned in a Despatch for Distinguished Service in Northern Ireland. I am charged to record Her Majesty's Highest Appreciation.

Our time in Omagh continued with many a varied task and incident until January 1993. January 1993 saw my promotion to corporal at the young age of 21, the youngest in the battalion. It was at this time that I had received my next posting order, a posting that from the day I passed out from my basic training, I always wanted to do. I was now being posted to the Infantry Training Battalion at Ouston, Newcastle as an Instructor to train

Darren (left) with 'Chalky' White (centre) during his time
training recruits in Newcastle in 1993.

army recruits for two and a half years. When I did my basic training I always looked up to the instructors and thought that I would always want to do what they were doing to me, but most importantly I wanted to train recruits to be trained soldiers, which to me was a massive achievement. And once back in battalion the qualification would enable me to practice trained soldiers in infantry skills and weapons and to train them in new tactics.

January 23rd 1993 was the day I reported for work and to my surprise, the platoon sergeant was 'Chalky' White – my section commander when I was a young recruit only five years earlier at Winchester. Now that we were NCOs in the same role, our relationship was completely different.

I spent those two and a half years training recruits and enjoyed it very much and did a job that gave me so much pride and self satisfaction. Yes recruits were beasted, it happened to me and I did it to them, but that is part and parcel of military training and it builds strength, discipline and character and many other skills and abilities that are required in the battlefield and on operations. At the platoon piss-up every 12 weeks after the recruits joined it was mostly enjoyable, and I felt they left with the same positive attitude that I did when I completed my training. It was hard, easy and enjoyable but the NCOs were there to do a job. Hopefully they left to pursue the same success as I.

As part of this training, many weeks were spent on exercise at various local locations, in particular Otterburn where we spent the last two weeks on final exercise. It was an area of vast barren moorland which afforded a variety of live firing ranges to practice live shooting skills and at the end of that the area was used for tactical training.

Whilst in a patrol base in a dense wooded area the platoon commander addressed the four section commanders with a warning order to warn the sections of the night time reconnaissance patrols that were to be deployed. But before he did that he said: "Corporal Ware, what have you done for meritorious service in Northern Ireland?" "What do you mean boss?" "What have you done for merit in Northern Ireland?" I paused, thought and again said "What do you mean?" He then said "I don't know what you have done, but you have just been awarded a Mention in Dispatches for distinguished service in Northern Ireland in the Operational Honours and Awards List, the company commander wants to see you".

It gave me immense pride that I had been awarded some recognition for the terrorist incident in April 1992. A few weeks later the award arrived at the Infantry Training Battalion and I was summonsed in front of the Commanding Officer to accept my certificate of citation and a bronze oak leaf to be attached to my Northern Ireland medal. That was it as far as I thought, but to my surprise I then began to receive letters from a very important high-ranking officer from across the army.

The first I received was from Brigadier Farrar-Hockley MC, the Directorate of Infantry Training, who commanded the Parachute Regiment in the Falklands War. Amongst other things his letter read:

I know that these awards are not made lightly and that yours reflects an outstanding tour of the Province as a section commander with your battalion.

The next was from Major General Freer, Commander of Land Forces Northern Ireland:

I am very pleased that your leadership and professionalism throughout your tour of Omagh, exemplified by the incident on 3rd April 1992 which resulted in the arrest of a terrorist, has been recognised in this way, well done.

From Lt Colonel Cottam OBE, my commanding officer at the time:

Many, many congratulations on your award of a Mention in Dispatches. That little oak leaf means so much; you thoroughly deserve it for your courage and leadership shown in Northern Ireland.

Lt General Sir Peter Duffle KCB CBE MC wrote:

I am delighted to see that you have been awarded a Mention in Dispatches in the Northern Ireland list. I am very pleased to see a member of the army training organisation recognised in this way.

From Brigadier Palmer, the Brigade Commander of 8 Infantry Brigade Northern Ireland:

A very well done on your award of a Mention in Dispatches in the operational honours and awards list. Although you were clearly a committed, loyal and professional patrol commander throughout your two year tour, it was your actions on the 3rd April 1992 for which you were particularly cited. In recognising a terrorist, who was not well known, and having the moral courage to pursue your suspicion with determination, you undoubtedly foiled an attempt to murder members of the security forces. You can take the credit for the subsequent conviction of that terrorist.

The RUC Divisional Commander wrote to my CO:

As you are aware an 8 man foot patrol under the command of LCpl Ware detained a suspect in Church Street Strabane. Follow up action revealed a concealed IED in a building. The excellent work performed by your soldiers on this occasion should not go unnoticed. There is no doubt that the professionalism of the patrol successfully disrupted a terrorist 'operation' and saved lives. The actions of your soldiers were commendable.

The Divisional Commander of the Light Division Training Depot, Colonel Williams, wrote:

I was really delighted to find your name highlighted today in the list of those awarded a Mention in Dispatches as a result of your recent time in Northern Ireland. The award is a great honour for both you and the Regiment not to mention the Division and you have every right to feel very proud.

General Jones KCB CBE, the Colonel Commandant of the Royal Green Jackets:

It gives me the greatest possible pleasure to congratulate you on your Mention in Dispatches as a result of your recent tour with the 1 RGJ in Omagh. Not only is it a significant achievement for you but it is also a great honour and your many friends in the battalion and throughout the Regiment will be as delighted as I am. Many congratulations and well done.

Finally, the most comforting letter was from my Company Commander at the time, a personal one to me:

Well done you. It was the greatest pleasure to read of your Mention in Dispatches in the Northern Ireland list. Your skill and professionalism on that dark distant night in Strabane undoubtedly disrupted a terrorist attack against the security forces which, had it been successful, would have resulted in injury and perhaps loss of life. I am delighted for you and your family.

Deservedly, the Company Commander received the MBE as a reward for his command and control as a reflection of A Company's performance and success in those two years. Both his and my recognition is a personal one.

I rejoined the battalion in July 1995 during the last few months of the two year posting to Dhekelia, Cyprus. The thought of a five month posting to Cyprus suited until we arrived there to find that our army quarter was a first floor flat in Larnaca, four miles from the garrison and stuck in a Cypriot-populated area with no one else that we knew nearby, and every couple of weeks I was away on operations on the border for ten days at the time. I did not enjoy it either and found an early escape back to Bulford as part of the pre-advance party in December 1995. My driving experience as an APC driver was my get out of jail free card, as the company had to supply such drivers to return to Bulford to collect the new fleet of vehicles. Some were not happy but who cares, I wasn't happy there and I was glad to get back to the UK having had a five month 'holiday'.

January 1996, the complete battalion had returned from embarkation and Christmas leave to Bulford to undertake the role of a mechanised infantry battalion. In February 1996 my daughter was born and in August 1996 we were off to Bosnia for a six month tour, and it was to be a busy year to face. It was during this nine month period that I was to change my mind about the army and my decision to leave – but not before an operational tour of Bosnia was complete.

August 2nd 1996 was a hard day. I left my army flat having said goodbye to my family and four month old daughter who did not know me. Later on that night I flew from RAF Brize Norton to Split, Croatia, arriving by late evening on the hot and sunny coastal resort mostly unaffected by the Bosnian war. A coach journey took us deep into central Bosnia, having crossed the checkpoint border crossing from Croatia into Bosnia situated high in the mountain region. By this time darkness had fallen and there was nothing to see what we were entering into. Our arrival at the 'Tom Factory' in Gornji Vakuf was the start of a military operation which began about 2am. We said goodbye to the 'comfortable' coach and loaded our kit onto the back of a four tonne truck and drove the short journey to our company location at the 'Precision Factory' in Gornji Vakuf. In the time of economic strength before the war it was a productive steel factory, but now run-down it provided our base for the next four months. The accommodation was a load of ISO containers of 4 man rooms and a short walk to the separate toilets and washrooms. Inside the main buildings, although it was small, it provided a gym and a couple of small bars and restaurants to afford some snack bars and relief from the company lines.

The battalion formed part of the NATO Implementation Force, known as IFOR, whose role post-war was to ensure the Dayton Peace Agreement was met and the General Framework Agreement for Peace between all warring factions of Serbs and Croats were met.

We dominated the AOR with mainly mobile patrols and occasional foot patrols in the nearby towns of Gornji Vakuf and Burgonio. The first day was spent on familiarisation patrols of the towns and surrounding area, an experience which was an eye opener. Our arrival overnight was masked by the darkness as the street lighting and visibility was very poor, if non-existent. Our first patrol was in daylight and I was shocked to see the devastation of the area and the poverty that followed the war. Most buildings were bullet-ridden, bombed out or derelict. People were still living in houses that had shell damage or had been shot to pieces, and due to economical weakness had no choice but to carry on living their lives there.

Any area off the main roads was strictly out of bounds as most rural areas were minefields not cleared after the war, which was evident with overgrown foliage and a variety of warning signs. A lot of the mines could be seen from the roadside and on river beds and on a daily basis you would hear the occasional mine detonation as locals endeavoured to return to normality to make a living and taking the risk to re-enter farming fields only to step on or walk over mines.

The destroyed village of Baptista, Gornji Vakuf, Bosnia in 1996.

Our tasking was mainly twofold. Operations consisted of mobile and foot patrols and manning the local International Police Task Force station at Burgonio and foot patrols in the town to reassure the local population. Accompanied by an interpreter our task was ensure the Dayton Peace Agreement was met, reassure the locals and to conduct checks on local military establishments ensuring they were not holding more weapons than they should. Our operational experience was very much an eye opener to see how people of Eastern Europe suffered and survived a civil war.

Almost every one of the patrols that I led my section on was an experience, an eye-opener and of interest. The use of the interpreter was helpful as I found it useful and interesting to mix and speak with local population and residents, to listen to their stories and experiences of the war and how they felt about a military presence in their country. I had been keen to do a similar thing in Northern Ireland but that had not been so easy. We were received very well by most people in Bosnia and often invited in for a strong coffee and soon realised that the way of life, the Government and the awful experience of what they had experienced over the years was immense. I drove through the village of Batista on the outskirts of Gornji Vakuf which had been completely destroyed and deserted and having drove the half mile through it we re-entered the main town.

Another patrol took me from Gornji Vakuf to Burgonio, passing many large farmers' fields, many of which were overgrown, an indicator that they were minefields, and because they were not used it caused them to become over grown. Other similar fields were marked with improvised signs warning of 'Minarano' – a minefield. In most of these fields I saw workers using basic hand tools to tend to their fields and growth, mainly cabbages, to earn money to make a living. It was not uncommon to hear the occasional explosion, hoping that nobody was harmed, but soon to learn that another farmer was killed or injured in a desperate attempt to make a living. One afternoon I was tasked by the Intelligence Unit to visit and patrol a remote village south east of Burgonjio that had not been visited before, so that an assessment could be done on its occupancy, accessibility and intelligence.

The captured AK47 assault rifle I seized from the Muslim gunman in the remote village north of Burgonio - my second successful operational achievement.

My section vehicle, commanded by me, left the main road and drove onto a narrowing track that led up to the hilltop village. I had identified a place to stop the APC as I knew that the remainder of the track had not been used by military vehicles, and due to the mine threat I decided to stop and assess the ground in front. Although there were one or two dwellings that were inhabited it was clearly not suitable for a 12 tonne APC. Having made my appreciation I decided to patrol to the remote village on foot and take with me a team of four – myself, my driver who was one of the most experienced soldiers on my team, one other Rifleman and my interpreter, Jasmin. I left behind my second-in-command plus four men, of whom one could drive. There was no need to leave my driver with the vehicle as it could not be brought forward, and that was the reason why I wanted to take the experience with me.

What confronted me I had not expected and what made it more difficult was that communications between me and my second in command had failed due to the terrain, and there was no possible way that I could contact them to bring the vehicle up to us or to send a runner back to bring them forward on foot. I did not want to send a lone Rifleman half a kilometre to bring reinforcements, leaving just me and one other with an unarmed interpreter.

Out of the wooded area to my right and about 10 metres in front of me walked two adult males both of whom were wearing combat clothing, neither of them had seen us, and one of them was carrying a Kalashnikov AK47 assault rifle. I dropped to my knees, and instructed the others to go firm. There was next to no immediate cover to take for our own protection, my heart immediately began to beat extremely fast and in a fraction of a second or two, I had to ascertain whether they were the only two. I had to protect myself and my team, I reached over to my assault rifle with my left hand and cocked it, loading a round into the chamber, placed the weapon into my right shoulder and issued a firm warning in Serb Croat "IFOR, STANI ILLI PUT SAM". Translated into English this clearly states "IFOR stand still or I will shoot". The middle-aged man turned in my direction and fortunately for him with the weapon to his side began to ramble in unrecognisable language. He made no immediate threat, and if he had levelled the AK47 towards us then he would have been shot. The male was verbally challenged in an aggressive but firm manner and disarmed at gun-point. The situation was not easy. The male did not want to surrender the weapon but I wanted it, and I needed him to give it to me.

The rest of my section was not aware of what as going on and the incident took probably three quarters of an hour to resolve. Once I had seized the AK47 from him we made our way back to the rest of the section and made a swift return to base having radioed through with a situation report. I was immensely impressed as to how our section had dealt with this incident and received several deserved verbal commendations and some sarcastic abuse, as you would expect!

During the much publicised and important General Elections our platoon was located as a reserve force in a disused car park near to the bombed-out derelict hospital at Burgonio. Our task was a QRF for any incident and under strict orders not to deploy unless ordered. The early evening surprise of a bomb attack at our location disturbed me as I sat beside my APC writing a set of orders. The large explosion caused no casualties apart from seriously pissing off a load of Green Jackets, who could not locate the terrorist responsible.

We were to learn that soon after the elections, the Government had been restructured and thereafter we were to learn that our tour was to be cut short and our return to UK to be earlier than expected. This was a great feeling, but also one of disappointment, as the time in Bosnia was a very good experience. My R&R was programmed for the end of the year but due to the recent announcement to return early, all R&R was cancelled, which meant that although some had gone home on R&R, our tour was four months without a visit home.

After this point I looked back on the achievements of my operational career and realised that having been sent to Northern Ireland I had achieved my aim and been awarded a Mention in Dispatches. I had then been sent to Bosnia and had also achieved our aim as part of the Dayton Peace Agreement and been commended for that too. Having realised that there was not much more I could achieve with my previous operational experience I decided in late 1996 to hand my notice in and leave the army. I was to serve 12 more months and in November 1996 the complete Battalion returned from Bosnia and back to Bulford. In the last 12 months of my army career I wanted an easier life and I felt that after 9 year's service I could do with 'winding down'. I had asked to be posted to the Training Wing as my instructor qualifications of Infantry Tactics, Infantry Weapons, Nuclear Biological and Chemical Warfare and a Small Arms Trainer Custodian would put me to good use.

The last year was spent trying to buy myself a house and to get myself another good career. In February 1997 I moved into my first owned home in East Lancashire and in

September 1997 my final days in the army were numbered. I had a final interview with my Company Commander thanking me for my services and right up to the eleventh hour again was offered promotion to Sergeant as an incentive to change my mind and stay in.

The carrot was dangled too often but I did not take it. My last official farewell interview was with the Company Sergeant Major and he ended by saying "I'll see you in six months". Because I was a keen soldier and well-qualified he had expected me to re enlist after a few months and thought I would not settle into civilian life, but he was to be wrong.

Six months after leaving the army I was to be employed as a police officer with the Police service and never looked back. Though I must admit I do miss the social and operational life in Northern Ireland, Bosnia and Cyprus I put the army behind me and moved on.

2

Blood brother

Born on 23rd January 1969 in South Lodge Hospital, North London, Simon was the first son to our parents Dennis and Lesley. He had not been born into a family home, as mum and dad had only married the year before, so his first home was in Shirley Road, in an end-terraced house in Enfield, the house that our grandmother lived in, which was a stepping-stone to the first family home. In 1970 mum and dad moved a mile or so across to the other side of town, to St Andrew's Road. This was a large semi-detached house with a lot more space for the family to live and grow up in, and more importantly for my dad, without the live-in mother-in-law. The house was brought from our Aunty Edna, Dad's sister, for £2,000, which I suppose in 1970 was an average price for the time and a cheap deal to seal. It was a large house, with a basement that was not my favourite place to visit. Tenants Phoebe and Bill who were living there when Edna had the house, occupied the ground floor; they were a retired couple who kept themselves to themselves really, but there were times when I would witness mum having a verbal argument with Phoebe on one or two occasions, but I was never to know the story behind it.

The first floor level had the kitchen, bathroom, living room and dining room, with the top floor having the two bedrooms. My memories of the house are that of a large one, but that was in my early years of recollection and I left the house when I was eleven and never returned, not through my own choice. Many a time over the years I returned for a drive past just to reminisce and I would still see it as it was, with the distinctive orange front door and front brick wall with tall pillars on each side, which enclosed the garden. It would have been so nice just to knock on the door and ask to have a look around but I thought it would be cheeky and felt a bit concerned as to what response I might have got.

On the 3rd March 1971 I was born in the upstairs front bedroom of the house, the second and last son that our parents had to put up with. The two of us grew up together in this house for many years and Simon and I had a good relationship together, but no doubt like many other brothers, we had our fights and were also a handful for our parents from time to time. We had many friends each over the years, many of whom had brothers of similar ages whom we associated with, the likes of Charlie and Anthony Wynne, Stephen and Robbie White and Ian and John Richards, to name but a few.

Dad was a self-employed painter and decorator and being young I didn't take much notice of what his business was all about as he got up early and went to work. The only thing I remember was his small dark blue car, a Ford Escort Mark 1 van full up with tools, brushes, paint and stepladders in the back. The old blue Ford escort van soon went and dad bought a family car, which was a bright red Ford Cortina estate Mark 2 and my good memory for numbers still recalls the registration number as VMV 364M – no doubt it is now dead and buried. Mum was an office secretary for Thorn EMI, a large well-known electrical company where she worked for many years.

Our education and upbringing was working class and we attended St George's Roman Catholic Primary School, Gordon Road in Enfield. Simon was two years above

St Andrew's Rd, Enfield – the house where the author was born and grew up with Simon.

me and he was an influence, I looked up to him as my 'Big Brother'. We did many things together and even belonged to the same Scout group, which used to meet at St George's school hall every Friday evening. We would leave home that little bit early in order to get up to mischief particularly in the summer evenings, but not in a criminal way. We lived about two miles away so none of the school neighbours knew us to complain to our parents. One Friday night near to firework night we brought some rockets from a nearby local newsagent, who would quite happily sell fireworks to under 16's in those days. The strict law enforcement these days was not as effective in the 80's. We had the matches with us so that it wasn't too obvious. On one side of the school playground there was a small drinking fountain on the wall, which was adjacent to the Headmaster's office and opposite the infant classrooms about 30 metres away. Simon and I set a rocket off horizontally from the fountain towards the other side of the playground but little did we know that one of them would go straight through a classroom window, which was not our intention! Knowing that none of the neighbours noticed, we left it. Much to our surprise we discovered that during school assembly on Monday morning from the head teacher, Mr. Groves, that not only had the rocket that caused the damage but he also had a witness that stood up and put mine and Simon's name forward as those responsible – bastard!

Simon and I would meet up at break times but there were times when he would want to be with his mates and he wouldn't want pestering and there were times when I was the same. When he was 11, Simon left St George's and went to the secondary school at St Ignatius College, Slades Hill, about five miles away. There was a two-year gap until I joined the same school in 1982. There we were again at the same school and by this time he and I had different school friends. It was a different school in all, as St George's was a mixed one and St Ignatius was an all boys' school and a lot stricter, which was a positive sign.

Unbeknown to us, mum and dad's marriage was going through a rough patch, and by the beginning of 1982 they had separated, and later divorced. It was by this time that I realised the reason why there was bedding folded up on the bed settee in the living room. It was because mum was using it to sleep on in the absence of a spare room. I had the awkward task of telling my friends, although it was fairly common in those days for parents to get divorced. I remember telling my best mate Stevie White one morning before school that my parents were separating and he just laughed, which resulted in a swift slap from his mother. After all he was only getting his own back when I laughed at him when his parents split up a few years earlier. I never did know the reason why mum and dad split only a few years earlier. I had decided to move out and live with mum about four miles away, while Simon remained at St Andrew's Road with dad. I didn't know exactly why I went with mum but I think there was an agreement that mum and dad should have one of us each and I don't think Simon wanted to go so I suppose it was only fair that I went. This made our time apart even greater and I only tended to see Simon at the weekends, apart from those brief occasions at school. Mum was pretty strict when it came to the schooling week and insisted only on visiting local friends, and I only tended to see Simon and dad at the weekend. I remember the day when mum moved out and my grandparents were helping her move into the new house. I went to school that day in the normal way and mum told me to go and say goodbye to dad, and to tell him that I would see him at the weekend. I went upstairs to his bedroom, he was still in bed but awake. After all, he had nothing to get up for. The fact that it was the day his wife was leaving him was not an incentive to get up. In hindsight it was the day that began the story of his final few years. It was an unmotivated period of time for him, with a certain level of depression that had some effect on his health and ultimately a contribution to his dying, partly of a broken heart. I gave him a kiss and said "I'll see you at the weekend". I was eleven years old and didn't know too much to show any emotions and was naive, I suppose at that young age – boys of that age don't know how to show emotions sometimes. If I knew then about how I feel now and what I knew at the time, then I would have spent as much time as possible with Simon and dad. Hindsight is a wonderful thing.

Mum had moved out for a fresh start in another three-bedroomed house. She had me, she had her new partner and she still had her job, the quality of life that my father did not have and I feel so sorry for him, he didn't have much. Mum's new house in Clarence Road, Ponders End was to be my new home for the next five years – it was a three-bedroomed house with a front and back garden and a double garage at the back. The ground floor consisted of an open plan staircase and dining room through to the living room and separate kitchen to the left. The first floor simply consisted of the three bedrooms and bathroom and my room was bedroom two and situated at the rear of the house.

The next few years were difficult. I could tell there was an atmosphere between dad and me and at times he made me feel intimidated, but he was never nasty. I could tell that all he wanted was a complete family and not a divorce or a separated life and I felt that part of that was my fault although I never knew why, I suppose it was a feeling of guilt. It even got to the stage where at times I was avoiding him. Being brought up in a Catholic school, dad insisted I went to church service every Sunday and I had to meet him at the church prior to the service starting, but there were times when I would attend an earlier service and go home. It even spread to dad's mum, when I got the blame for my mum allegedly digging up the daffodil bulbs when she left St Andrew's Road. It transpired that they were only 'annuals' so they didn't grow after the first year. The situation worsened for dad and his business wasn't good and he soon stopped working. I don't know how that materialised but he began to spend most of his time at the local church hall where he did voluntary work maintaining and running the bar and social club. He even cooked and ate there, I guess to save money on his own fuel bills at home. In the end dad began to spend a lot of time at the church bar and social club and even parked the Ford Cortina there. It never moved for months and began to get even dirtier parked under a large willow tree.

The tree sap and bird droppings soon took its toll on the paintwork and it soon got all its windows smashed and then scraped.

I used to meet dad regularly on a Saturday lunchtime, when he always cooked tomato soup and bread, the cheapest option I suppose, and a few free beers for me when he cleaned the pipes out. I was the 'guinea pig' who tested the first clean pint, which always tasted fine to me and it made me tipsy after a few.

A milestone in Simon's life now arrived in August 1985 when he left school and joined the army. This was an occasion I was really proud of. Word soon spread around the school that "Darren Ware's brother had joined the army," an event that was seldom heard of and I was asked regularly how he was and what he was up to. Because he was a Coldstream Guardsman, the thought of him doing ceremonial duties outside Buckingham Palace, Clarence House, St James' Palace and Windsor Castle created more interest. At that time he wasn't just any soldier – he was a Guardsman and he would soon be outside Buckingham Palace, wearing his red tunic with buttons in two's and black bearskin with a single red plume on the right side.

Simon completed his basic training and passed out in February 1986, having completed five months of arduous basic training at the Guards Depot at Pirbright in Surrey. He was one of the youngest adult recruits who formed Number 10 Platoon, Caterham Company. Mum wrote a letter to school to get me the day off school to attend Simon's Passing-out Parade and Mr. Lawrence, my form teacher, granted it. I was really excited at attending his passing out parade and spoke about it to everyone that I could. The parade was impressive, but was marred by wind and rain, but the soldiers battled on. Although spectators were sheltered, it couldn't have been nice for the boys on parade. I still have the occasional look at the video of 10 Platoon, Caterham Company passing out. It was an hour's display of professional, exemplary precision drill conducted by soldiers famous for it all over the world.

I was in the cadets and was soon to join the army. I was proud of him and looked forward to the day I joined the army myself.

Simon joined the 1st Battalion Coldstream Guards and off he went to his first posting to Stanley Fort, Hong Kong, for at least 12 months. It seemed like ages until he returned. He didn't return home on leave whilst in Hong Kong so we only contacted one another by letter. I don't think he phoned that often. Having an overseas posting to Hong Kong at the age of 17 and single meant that he had no need to come home.

Simon returned near to the end of 1987 and by this time I had joined the Royal Green Jackets at 16 and was doing my basic training at Sir John Moore Barracks at Winchester, The Light Division Training Depot. It was only opened the year before as a brand new training depot for recruits of the Light Infantry and the Royal Green Jackets, who form the Light Division. I came home on leave from time to time and met up with Simon as often as I could. Now we were both in the army we saw each other as often as we could. As I neared the end of my basic training there was a chance of being posted to Gibraltar with the 3rd Battalion The Royal Green Jackets. This would have meant less time together with Simon but fortunately I was posted to the 2nd Battalion and based at Warminster, Wiltshire in July 1988. The battalion was earmarked to go to Northern Ireland in February 1989 on a four and a half month tour of County Fermanagh and as the battalion was off on an operational tour most new recruits were sent to boost the numbers.

Simon in his Number Two suit the week after his passing-out parade.

Sadly and tragically the shock news of our father's death occurred on 8th March 1988, he died of a sudden heart attack in his sleep. I remember being in the toilets one morning when another recruit asked me where my nearest railway station was for a train warrant to get home on leave. The platoon had been given an extra weekend off to go home but I wasn't bothered, as I wanted to stay at Winchester with the lads. I told the recruit I didn't need a train warrant but I was soon called to the NCOs office and received a condolence pat on the back by Corporal 'Jimmy' Joynt, although I did not realise what was to happen. The Platoon Commander called me into his office and said to me, "Brace yourself, I have some bad news. Your father had a heart attack, he died last night." I was numbed with shock and did not know what to say. I had only turned 17 five days earlier and was still a juvenile. I have only left home three months ago and I did not know what to do or say. I just needed and wanted to be home with my family, my brother, my mother, my aunts and my girlfriend so that I could seek guidance from them as to 'what happens now'. Looking back, it must have been the stress of his divorce and business running down that made him die of a broken heart. The Platoon Commander asked if he had suffered an illness, and I said that he had. In his own way he had really since mum left him. We were both away and could not have foreseen the day-to-day depression or downfall. Unbeknown to us he did have a girlfriend for some time, she was called Kit, so at least he had some company and happiness. Dad's death brought Simon and I even closer together. Shortly after this, in April 1988, mum and her partner Terry (who later became my step-father) moved to Norfolk and settled down to their retirement in a bungalow in a nice quiet cul-de-sac in Holt.

Most of my leave and weekends off were spent in London. I was on my second posting and based at Dover with the 2nd Battalion The Royal Green Jackets. I spent my leave at Charlie's house, in Enfield as a roof over my head. Charlie was a good friend who later was to be my Best Man at my wedding. His father, Louis and step-mum Delia, put up with me after many nights on the piss in the Enfield Arms and I never really thanked them both for the inconvenience I caused. I know I did cause an inconvenience because I recall being sick one night all over the floor of their brand-new fitted kitchen. Fortunately Charlie was behind me to clean up the mess. There were other incidents, no doubt.

Many a time I met up with Simon and his mates on regular visits to the famous Duke of York public house on Victoria Street, Victoria, just around the corner from Wellington Barracks – a good haunt. I felt I wanted to be with Simon to obtain the knowledge and gain influence from him about army life and what being a 'squaddie' was all about. That's where I met a few of his mates, 'Fen' to name but a few. "He's got a gun!" and everyone went for cover – this was one of Fen's quotes, from the Schwarzenegger film Total Recall, it was one of those army things and it looked good. Many a good night was had by all.

The Duke of York Tavern, Victoria Street, London – just around the corner from Wellington Barracks and the 'local haunt' for the off-duty guardsmen.

With mum outside Wellington Barracks in June 1990, after Simon's first Trooping the Colour.

Simon later met Carol, who was a nurse, and he soon moved into her flat in Shepherd's Bush, when they then began to use another drinking hole – *The Three Tuns* in Marble Arch. It was a small pub just behind a main road, which seemed popular and with a bit of character. One night we saw Adam Woodyatt, who plays Ian Beale in *Eastenders* in there.

In September 1988 Simon had gone to Belfast for four and a half months on his first tour, based at the North Howard Street Mill. Mum began to worry, until his safe return in February 1989, by which time I had gone on a four and a half month tour of County Fermanagh, based at Lisnaskea and operating close to the border. So mum was panicking for eight months in all! Fortunately both tours were quiet and uneventful so it reassured her. Well, that's what we told her anyway.

In the summer of 1989 Simon took part in his first Trooping the Colour. His involvement at this time was street-lining The Mall. He was excited and proud to have taken part in it. The following year he took part in his second Troop on the 16th June 1990 and with a little more involvement. The 1st Battalion Coldstream Guards were responsible for forming part of Number 6 Guard so we all got tickets and went to watch. Of course we couldn't pick him out from the hundreds of red tunics and bearskins even though we knew he was the centre man in the front rank. It was a thoroughly impressive performance and it was obvious that a lot of work and practice went into it.

Afterwards mum, Terry, Simon, Carol and I met up and went to a local pub, The Feathers, next to St James' Park tube station, for some beers and food. Mum took this opportunity to tell us that she had been recently diagnosed with breast cancer, which was malignant. Shocked! Unbeknown to us a lump she had removed a year or so earlier was benign and I think she must have realised that this time there was no way of fighting it, so she had to tell us. I didn't know what to say really, Simon was shocked. There had never been cancer in the family that I knew of, so I didn't know what to expect.

A few months later in October 1990 Simon had transferred to the 2nd Battalion as the 1st battalion was going to Germany at the end of 1990 and that would have ruined his wedding plans for March 1991. Simon's battalion and mine had started training for Northern Ireland once again, ready for my deployment to Co. Tyrone for two and a half years and Simon's deployment to South Armagh for six months in March. This no doubt

The evening reception at Simon's wedding with a proud mum.

brought back all the worry for mum that she went through in 1989, making her illness worse.

On 3rd March 1991, my 20th birthday, I flew out to Northern Ireland and took up an operational role as the residential infantry battalion in the garrison town of Omagh, Co Tyrone. This was becoming a regular occurrence, as only some days after my 18th birthday the army kindly sent me to Northern Ireland on my first tour. Omagh was a lovely market town which appeared friendly, with plenty of shops and drinking holes. When I mentioned Omagh to friends and family they thought I was in Armagh. It wasn't until the tragic events on 15th August 1998, when 29 people were killed in a car bomb put Omagh on the map.

I came home for Simon and Carol's wedding a couple of days later as I was his Best Man on that day. On the 9th March they were married at the Guards Chapel, Wellington Barracks, followed by a reception in the Corporal's Mess and a night full of beer-fuelled party atmosphere. After the reception Simon and I got changed out of our uniform, as Simon had been in his red tunic ceremonial dress all day and I had worn my regimental number two suit, and we both wore identical dinner suits in the evening as Simon had wished.

There are so many memories that are brought back when I see old photographs and remember old thoughts and I start to feel the heart strings begin to tug and the tight feeling in my throat. I am sentimental but don't often cry and when I get the feelings I stop what I am doing and wander off for a short period. This book would have been written in half the time if I did not keep stopping and starting.

Two days later on March 11th I returned to Omagh. It was on this day too that Simon deployed with his battalion to South Armagh. We met up briefly at Belfast Aldergrove military airport as I waited for my transport back to Omagh having deliberately got there late so that I could meet Simon on his arrival in the morning. Because I deliberately missed it, I could not get any accommodation so I got my head down in the doorway of an aircraft hangar until first light. It was cold and uncomfortable but worth the wait to see Simon briefly. He was part of the baggage party waiting for transport to take the kit and equipment to Bessbrook.

As the next few months went on we were both busy on operations and concentrating on the job to hand. We contacted each other regularly on the phone and often exchanged 'war stories' of incidents that had happened or described what we were involved in.

Simon came home on his five days R&R on 23rd May 1991 and fortunately it was the same time I had a couple of weeks leave, having gone on leave on the 13th May. Simon's time at home was short and we met up as often as we could and worked around the time together he had with Carol, so when Carol was at work we met up. We talked 'shop' and talked about our experiences and there were two distinctive events in those five days. One was an all-day drinking session in one of his locals in Shepherd's Bush where he used to live. There was Carol, Rhiannon and Lindsey as well as a few of Simon's friends and we just drank and laughed all day. The other thing I recall was when we were going somewhere in London in a black cab, probably going on the piss. He told me that he was approached whilst on patrol by an Irish woman telling him that he would go home in a body bag, but comments like that were very common. Simon would always say that if he were to get killed then he would prefer it to be in an explosion, and then at least he wouldn't feel it and I tended to agree with him. If she ever knew what happened to him I wonder if she would have any true remorse, although I doubt it. Soon after that we both returned to Northern Ireland to get on with operations. Simon's tour was almost over while mine wasn't even a third of the way through.

At the end of July of 1991 our Company, A Company, deployed to Rockwood on another five weeks of operations and of course we contacted one another on a regular basis again. Simon tended to phone the Company Operations room to leave a message and I would then return the call. I remember distinctly a phone conversation on the 14th August. Our Company 2i/c was a bit aggrieved by Simon's regular calls to the operations room and told me to ask him to reduce them. That pissed me off, because I felt he was not very understanding over the situation of both of us being in Northern Ireland. After all, he was the RSM only a few years earlier and you wouldn't expect too much compassion from a soldier of that capacity. 'Rocky' was his nickname. Anyway I told Simon about what the 2i/c said but he wasn't bothered, his attitude being that if he had a problem then why didn't he speak to him! During this conversation Simon told me that his multiple was going on a three-day patrol. Obviously he didn't explain what he was doing, but would do once he returned. We ended the call and said 'keep your head down', something we always said as soldiers, which meant keep safe, and goodbye. For the last time! He never told me about that patrol, but I was to hear many stories from others about it.

3

'Grease your Gats'

I joined the Second Battalion The Royal Green Jackets, D Company 15 Platoon in July 1988 on my first posting to Battlesbury Barracks in Warminster, Wiltshire as part of the Infantry Trials and Development Unit (ITDU), and what a daunting and nervous experience that was. Depending on where your battalion was based it dictated the role for the duration of that posting and for Warminster the ITDU used the infantry battalion to trial and evaluate newly introduced military equipment from a wide range of themes.

I was a young 17 year old Rifleman new to the platoon and as such was subjected to the normal 'welcoming' process to the battalion that I expected most people would receive. Thankfully I had joined the platoon with at least two other recruits whom I trained with so I was not totally on my own, although there at best twenty five or so other riflemen in the platoon, all of whom were 'sweats' compared to me, thus making the ratio against me fairly high. Sharing a ten man room with other soldiers with more service than me was the 'norm' and being 'dicked' to do all the shit jobs was part of early life in the army in the 80's. I just could not wait for the next intake of new recruits to arrive so that the pressure could be taken off me, but that would not be a long time coming.

Whilst new to the training environment at the training depot we were referred to as 'sprogs' or 'crows' (combat recruit of war), but now that I was in the battalion that changed to 'nig' (new intake group) and you could end up being a 'nig' for six or twelve months. Having to make the brews, iron NCO's uniform uniforms and do other mundane crap jobs like going to the shops for them, or getting a take-away was what I was told to expect, and they were the easy tasks.

Back in the 80s there were the 'sweats' of the platoon, who were the senior Riflemen with several years' service under their belt, and if they had already completed a tour of Northern Ireland then they were even more of one and tougher in attitude and experience, which was common in those days. It was these 'sweats' that would expect the 'nigs' to do all the chores for them and it seemed a long climb up that ladder. I would often be woken from my sleep late at night to the sound of drunken 'sweats' returning from a night 'on the piss' and I did not expect to get back to sleep and over several months, though not every day, but particularly at weekends, I would be woken up to be inconvenienced. It was the nature of squaddies to go drinking, even during the week before the next day's work. It was part of army lifestyle, particularly for those single soldiers living on camp. The following weekday morning the drunken squaddies would turn up on parade somewhat worse for wear but managed to get through the day, sometimes I wondered how.

On one occasion I had a large tyre rolled over me whilst I was 'asleep' in bed by one of the notorious 'sweats' of the platoon then to be forced out of bed to make the brews. I later witnessed the same 'sweat' drag someone out of bed and attempt to throw one of the 'nigs' from a first floor window, thankfully he was prevented from doing so by some sensible blokes. It was a good job Simon had warned me of this type of behaviour, but I knew it would not last. Another time I was met by a senior Rifleman who had been put on the duties for a 24 hour barrack guard and told me that he was not doing it, so I suggested he spoke to one of the senior NCOs to sort it out, but I had obviously misunderstood him. He told me that I was doing it and short of getting a beating I suppose I had to do it and accept it.

However, not all were sensible; I don't know if it was a Green Jacket mentality or a general mentality for squaddies but some were mad and would do almost anything dangerous, and I mean anything. It wasn't until 1994 that three Green Jackets killed a Danish tour guide in Cyprus in 1994 in Ayia Nappa. It was truly shocking, I knew all three of those responsible but one in particular, more so than the other two; it was a tragic event which not only marred British soldiers in Cyprus but marred the good name of the Royal Green Jackets.

The posting to Warminster, when I joined the battalion, was nearing the end and Connaught Barracks in Dover was on the horizon in August 1988. Whilst in Warminster I was aware the battalion would be off to Northern Ireland at the beginning of 1989; after all it was for this reason that my initial choice of joining the Third Battalion and going off to Gibraltar was scrapped. I was soon to learn that we were to be posted to Belfast for a four and a half month tour and would be taking over from the 1st Battalion Coldstream Guards in February 1989. This was great news as I knew that Simon's battalion was deploying to Belfast in September 1988 and that we would relieve them and I had an advantage that I could share. I could get the information and intelligence and the 'full SP' from him on the patch we were going to. The highs and lows, the good and bad places and a whole host of knowledge that could help me get through. I mentioned this to several people in the platoon and Company who felt confident I had some inside information and it soon spread around that Rifleman Ware had an older brother in the army who we were taking over from in Northern Ireland. Though this was something that I did not wish to advertise so early on in my battalion life, I soon earned a bit more respect and was not really looked upon as a 'nig' so much.

As the build-up to Northern Ireland continued within the battalion and the platoon, we were informed that we were not now going to Belfast to relieve the Coldstream Guards but in fact now going to County Fermanagh to relieve 42 Commando Royal Marines. Because the Company locations in Fermanagh were close to the border the threat level was increased somewhat and the message was clear – it was officially announced on the Company Orders "We are off to Fermanagh, so grease your gats". This meant that the emphasis was on the possibility of some action so we were warned to make sure our weapons were well-oiled. Many soldiers in the battalion had gone to Northern Ireland before, all of the NCOs in the platoon had, but for the majority of the Riflemen this would be a new experience.

The battalion spent about four months on Northern Ireland training which taught us all the skills and abilities which were needed to survive. It taught us patrol skills and formations both for foot and vehicle patrols, how to enter and exit helicopters, how to react when known players were seen going about their own business. We were trained in contact drills should we get shot at or bombed, how to conduct rural and urban searches, house searches and the list went on. Having done all this and been tested to the max we were then ready to deploy. The battalion deployed to Fermanagh in February 1989, having flown out of RAF Lyneham, to take up four Company locations along the border region and have the responsibility of manning seven permanent vehicle checkpoints (PVCP's). D

The author on foot patrol in Rosslea, County Fermanagh, as
a young 18 year old Rifleman in 1989.

Company's three platoon locations were at Lisnaskea, Rosslea and Newtownbutler and the
Company was also responsible for the PVCP's at Wattlebridge, Kilturk, Annaghmartin
and Killivilly. When the battalion deployed I was only 17 and under military law soldiers
were not allowed to go to Northern Ireland until they were 18. Strange really, as only a
few years earlier in 1982 seventeen year old soldiers were fighting a war against Argentina
in the Falklands War, but it was the IRA murder of three 17 year old soldiers in Northern
Ireland in the 70's which changed the ruling. I turned 18 on March 3rd and a few days
later the army sent me to Northern Ireland – Happy Birthday! But I was not bothered
as I just wanted to get out there.

Amongst the routine, we had to man the PVCP's near the border so that we could
reassure the public, prevent the movement of guns, ammunition and explosives and disrupt
terrorist activity. Each PVCP was manned by a minimum of multiple strength and the
three four-man teams would rotate throughout, manning the checkpoint, sangar duties,
rest and quick reaction force (QRF), and those that were new to Northern Ireland and
new to battalion life, which was the category that I fell into, were then thrown into the
deep end.

Whilst at the Kilturk PVCP I was on my rest period when my section commander
told me to get my kit on and go and deal with a car at the search bay. I was told that a
known IRA 'player' had entered and his car needed searching and the details of all the
three passengers to be taken. I was also instructed to find out about their movements in
the hope of building an intelligence picture. This was my first encounter with a known
terrorist and it was daunting, though I was confident. I began speaking to him and I
expected him to answer simple questions which I put to him but he was not having any

of it. I obtained the details of the other occupants and the car but apart from that he was not telling me what he was up to. I then noticed that the rifleman on duty at the PVCP was doing the easy job of searching the car, and I was told to 'grill' the occupants, clearly being the harder job. It was then that I realised that these 'players' should be dealt with firmly and robustly. It was only a few weeks later at the same PVCP that 'Smudge' and I were checking vehicles when another 'player' entered in his vehicle in the early hours on his way to work. We proceeded to search his car and him, because that was what we could do. Under the Prevention of Terrorism Act and the Northern Ireland Emergency Provisions Act we did not have to give any reason, we just did it. There was nothing in his car, or on him, and we knew that most of these people would not be carrying guns or bombs because they knew they would get stopped and searched. But on this occasion we delved a little further and found his packed lunch box and searched that too. His sandwiches and salad was laid out on the bonnet of his car, his flask was opened and emptied out to ensure there was nothing illegal in it. As this was done we watched his coffee pour all over the road. I even opened a small Tupperware tub containing a white powdered substance, knowing that it was salt for his salad. The search procedure and conversation was recorded on my pocket Dictaphone and Smudge and I amused ourselves in the days following with other lads over the incident. My confidence was growing! Until we were made aware that the 'player' had complained to the police about the way he was treated at the checkpoint that morning. The police interviewed us both separately and seized my Dictaphone. They returned it some weeks later with a smile on their faces as they had found the incident amusing and had quashed his complaint – one nil to us!

Life in the PVCP was pretty dull really but you had to be alert all of the time, when you weren't on vehicle duties or sangar duties you would be expected to conduct mortar base plate patrols, or 'mortar flips' as they were referred to. This was a short patrol around the PVCP making sure that any vulnerable places that mortar attacks could be mounted from were clear. Mortar attacks in Fermanagh were high and only a few weeks before

On duty at PVCP 6 at Kilturk, County Fermanagh.

The cramped accommodation that we had to put up with so often.

we arrived the RUC station at Rosslea was attacked so we needed to make sure that the area was safe.

By this time in my early career I had now been recognised as being keen, responsible and tactically aware, so that I was given the responsible task of leading a four-man team on these 'mortar flips' which lasted about an hour. I felt trusted as I was only 18 and was given the responsibility of commanding short patrols in Northern Ireland.

That was life at the PVCP's, and only a few months after we were relieved, on the 13th December 1989, the checkpoint at Killyvilly was hit by a massive IRA attack, killing two soldiers. Once I read the incident report about the ferocity of the attack then I realised how lucky we were. Life was tough and the living conditions were cramped during that tour. Most occasions there were 12 of you with bunk beds three high in a room measuring 15 feet by 15 feet. Every few weeks the platoon would rotate around the three locations, causing you to basically live out of your kit bags and Bergen for most of the tour. Within those locations we would rotate around the PVCP's, and every so often specialist operations were planned and conducted; of course this would be dependant on operational incidents. On many occasions 'Eagle VCP's' would be conducted throughout the battalion area of responsibility. These were great as it involved airborne VCP's conducted on random roads over a vast area whilst flying around in helicopters being dropped off here, there and everywhere. The operations got even better; Operation Smack was a two-day boat operation on Upper and Lower Loch Erne speeding around in three high-speed rigid raiders containing four-man teams patrolling the Lochs for two days and conducting stop and searches on boats of all kinds that were using the waters. Most of them were law-abiding adventurists but there was always the terrorist threat of moving arms and ammunition across the water. Again, it was times like this that I placed myself in the position I was in – I was only 18 and in the army serving in Northern Ireland and being flown around in helicopters and speeding around in rigid raiding craft – I was the envy of all my mates.

A few weeks later the RUC station at Clogher was hit by machine gun fire from a drive-by shooting from an IRA active service unit on the back of a stolen flatbed truck

Waist deep in the swamp during the 8 mile route search to the terrorists'
vehicle at the border crossing point. I still had a smile on my face.

late one night. No casualties were inflicted but civilians in the area when the machine gun opened fire suffered shock and the police station was extensively damaged by the gunshots. Witnesses who observed the incident saw the vehicle head towards the border and out of sight. That night a planning and search operation was put in place and at first light the suspected vehicle was located at a border crossing point some 8 miles from the RUC station. Because our section was search-trained our multiple was tasked along with other search teams to conduct an eight mile route search from the contact point to where the vehicle had been abandoned just in case anything had been thrown from the vehicle as the terrorists escaped. The IRA being the sophisticated motivated individuals they are again executed the attack with minimal evidence being left behind. It was one of my longest and hardest days of that tour, we slogged through fields and hedgerows, hills and obstacles bouncing away from the road and bouncing back in every few hundred yards searching for discarded evidence and/or booby traps. It took us hours of hard work trying to search the route against time of light. We thought we had it tough but we passed static trench locations from troops from C Company who had been dug-in and were digging in all night to secure the area. We were looking at them thinking 'Thank god I wasn't digging in' and they were watching us probably thinking 'thank god we aren't doing the route search.' I have a picture of me waist-deep in a bog but with a smile on my face for whatever reason, we searched every part of that route as best we could but we found nothing. The ATO having declared the area safe thus allowed the RUC to move in to gather their evidence.

Close to Rosslea RUC station intelligence reports indicated that movement was being conducted across a nearby border crossing point through the night. A surveillance team had been authorised to place out technical equipment near to the crossing point to record any activity. Late one night, at short notice, our section was tasked with supporting the close surveillance operations team whilst they placed the surveillance equipment at the border crossing point. This involved a lot of OP's in that area with adrenaline going up and down when a mixture of humans and wildlife passed the technical equipment. We never caught anyone at the scene but were to learn some weeks later that video surveillance had picked up several sightings and activities by known players which led to further operations, weapons seizures and arrests, of course preventing and disrupting future terrorist operations.

That was as exciting as the Fermanagh tour got really, but during the tour we had been told that intelligence sources indicated that the Fermanagh Brigade of the IRA had been disbanded and I think from that, their actions dwindled.

Apart from terrorist operations, the joke was on me as it was my time to be in the limelight, though through no choice of mine. One of my early patrols from Lisnaskea forced me to negotiate a large barbed wire fence which was bigger than me. The fence got the better of my balancing attempt after which I fell off suffering a large laceration to the palm of my left hand caused by the barbed wire. I brushed it off as nothing serious but as the patrol continued I could not bear the pain of the injury and had to concede defeat and inform the patrol commander. The SF base was not too far away so we patrolled there to get myself stitched up and receive much abuse and piss-taking. On another occasion whilst at one of the PVCP's, food poisoning got the better of me and being safe in the knowledge that the food was not cooked by me I was evacuated by helicopter, embarrassingly, back to the Company location at Lisnaskea. Whilst at the PVCP's we were self-contained and had to do all the cooking and cleaning ourselves, I was so glad that I was not the victim of my own doing on this occasion. If it couldn't get any worse the next incident was even funnier and I could not blame anyone else. I had left my packing to go on R&R somewhat late in the day and had at the last minute grabbed a civvy bag from my locker and stuffed it full of clothes and stuff that I needed. On arrival at RAF Aldergrove, the military side of Belfast Airport, my bag went through the usual security checks during which a rifle magazine, thankfully empty, was detected on the x-ray machine. I remember seeing the image for myself and my heart just sank. I got gripped by the RMP's and told that I would be reported to my unit and no doubt disciplined on my return to Northern Ireland the following week – that set me up for a good R&R.

A few weeks later I was hauled in front of the Company Commander to be told of my fate, but fortunately for me as I had not been disciplined before he thought it not too serious and was lenient towards me. I was found guilty and given some stern words of advice and got more of a bollocking for not telling my platoon sergeant on return from R&R.

I left the Co. Fermanagh tour with no combat stories but I had gained plenty of experience, confidence and knowledge of Northern Ireland operations and sights of previous terrorist attacks and at the same time won some respect too. The battalion returned from Northern Ireland and were given four weeks leave. It had vastly opened my eyes to life, but at the same time I had a lot of stories to tell my friends back home and once I had been grilled in my local about what I had experienced at the age of 18 it attracted many more friends, particularly the female type. That was it, Fermanagh was over and after our leave we returned to duties in battalion. Time went on and within 12 months the battalion received a further warning order that it was to be deployed to Northern Ireland again.

No sooner had we returned to Dover in September 1989 then we were looking at being deployed to Omagh, Co Tyrone as the residential infantry battalion in March 1991 for two years. Having experienced the Fermanagh tour only 18 months earlier I had decided this time to keep a detailed written diary of my experiences. So 18 months earlier when I went to Fermanagh as a young inexperienced Rifleman with other NCO's having tours under their belt and me the new boy, here I was in March 1991 myself now an NCO with a previous tour of Fermanagh under my belt with new Riflemen in the position I was in only 18 months before. Within 18 months I had gone full circle and I was excited and raring to go again. However this time I ensured that the riflemen in my section and platoon who were inexperienced and not having been to Northern Ireland got the support and reassurance that they needed to prepare themselves.

On Sunday 3rd March 1991 on my 20th birthday I flew out from RAF Lyneham at 0620hrs to Belfast and then followed the noisy Chinook flight to Omagh in overcast weather conditions, which was typical weather for Northern Ireland. The battalion began to experience incidents right from the start. On the 10th March a patrol from D Company came under attack by an improvised anti-armour grenade (IAAG) in Strabane. There were no casualties but prior to the attack a woman had phoned the police informing them that she had seen two masked men in the Springhill Park estate. Clearly Strabane was going to be a busy town.

On the 18th March, after a tip off, an occupied house search was conducted by search teams from our company and I was tasked along with other teams to provide satellite support for the search operation in a house in Strabane. The search was successful with an amount of improvised landmines, a quantity of semtex and bomb making equipment being found and the operation resulted in the arrest of three terrorists. On Tuesday 2nd April 1991 at 0250hrs whilst executing my duties as the guard commander at Omagh a petrol bomb attack took place on one of the married quarter houses close to the perimeter and in view of the guard room. I deployed along with the fire picket and ran through the garrison with the heavy cumbersome fire cart. It was more of a horse-drawn cart with hoses and stand pipes and other fire fighting equipment, though it was not drawn by any horses just us and it was no easy task to get from A to B. By the time we arrived at the burning house and began to pump water the fire brigade turned up to do their job. I suppose for the sake of some energetic fitness then we got something out of it. Thankfully the house was unoccupied but was gutted by the fire; nobody was ever caught as the CCTV operator in the guard room only saw the two masked men disappear into the darkness.

On Sunday 13th April 1991 at 0237hrs RUC Castlederg informed the Ops room at Rockwood that they had received several calls of shots being heard in Killeen, two and a half miles south of Castlederg. A few moments later at 0249hrs reports confirmed that a fatal shooting had occurred against Ian Sproule outside his home address in Killeen. He had been brutally murdered by the IRA on his return from a disco. A total of 43 rounds were fired, with Ian being hit 37 times; he had no connections with the security forces but the IRA believed he was a member of the UVF/UDA. Following the shooting, at 0400hrs we were deployed as the QRF to assist the RUC cordon and search operation. The task was complete and the cordon was lifted at just after 1pm and once the scene was cleared we went to view the scene of the ghastly murder. Though Ian's body had been

The shooting of Ian Sproule in Killeen. Some of the many strike marks are clearly visible.

removed I observed the violent scene where the gunmen had sprayed the courtyard at the front of his house, as the bullet holes could be seen everywhere. Four days later we were drafted back to the Killen area following intelligence reports that a follow-up retaliation shooting was about to take place. Though it didn't we only hoped that we had foiled yet another murder by our sheer presence.

Shortly after midnight on the 30th June 1991 I was woken by the sound of a large explosion in Omagh. At the time I was the QRF commander and I quickly roused my section and made my way to the Ops room anticipating a deployment. Reports from the police filtered through that one of their mobile patrols had been involved in an explosion on the Mountfield Road. An RUC mobile patrol had been hit by a Mk 12 mortar attack

The construction of the Mk12 mortar. The mortar tube would often be laid on the ground and the projectile then fired horizontally at the target.

The Mk12 mortar attack on the RUC mobile patrol outside the Knock-Na-Moe Hotel in Omagh. Fortunately the tree took the brunt of it.

as it approached the entrance to the Knock-Na-Moe hotel. The device which was fired from the offside hit the bonnet of the police car, bounced off and hit a large tree where it detonated, sending shrapnel over the contact site. A following taxi was in the 'killing zone' and took the brunt of the explosion causing six casualties, one of whom was a police officer. We were the first army call-sign on the scene with the contact point still smouldering; I observed the large thick tree that took the mortar round with some destruction.

At 0630hrs on the 11th August 1991 whilst conducting operations as part of the Castlederg Ops Company we were deployed to reports of an explosion at a barn north of the town just off the Lurganbuoy Road. Initial reports suggested that a derelict barn had been booby-trapped so the usual planning and search clearance operation took place and we were tasked to ensure the area was patrolled and secure whilst the ATO did his job. At 1125hrs the following day the ATO had declared the area safe and confirmed that two explosions occurred, each being of between 100-200lb of semtex which took the form of a pressure pad device which had been activated by a herd of cows. This was another example of the terrorist ability to attempt to booby trap the security forces; the incident was declared a fatal explosion with the death of three cows.

On the 15th August 1991 an off-duty UDR soldier was shot dead south-west of Sion Mills as he was dropped off for work by his wife. This was a horrific and brutal murder when three masked men had opened fire with machine guns from a nearby hijacked house and once done so they made good their escape in a stolen car which was later found abandoned on the border, east of border crossing point 251 near Castlederg. At 1430hrs that day we were re-tasked back to Castlederg in preparation to relieve the call signs on the ground. Because the clearance operation was on the border we had no support from the Garda so that afternoon and most of the evening and into the night was spent digging trenches to protect ourselves. Whilst half of the platoon dug in, the other half conducted satellite patrols for protection. This would turn out to be one of my longest days and at

The barn explosion at Castlederg which caused the death of three cows.

1500hrs the following day the car was declared safe and recovered to RUC Strabane for forensic examination.

Apart from the terrorist incidents and pro-active search operations that took place, there were many occasions of verbal and physical abuse and sporadic scenes of disorder with an array of objects being thrown at us. During evening and night time patrols of the busy towns of Omagh, Strabane and Castlederg we were often met with chants and provocative comments from groups who just wanted to cause a fight or riot. On occasions we would often meet some of those individuals on their own when they were sober and they would act as though innocent and nice as pie, but revenge was sweet. On one particular night in Strabane whilst on foot patrol at about 4 am I received a call over the radio from my section 2 i/c to meet him. On my arrival I was met with an unconscious male on the floor whom I recognised as one of these gobby troublemakers. My 2i/c informed me that he had assaulted 'Bondy', who was one of my senior riflemen, and they had both ended up fighting. It had caused a gathering of 'witnesses' who all claimed the soldier had beaten him into unconsciousness. The police soon arrived and one of them told me that it could not have happened to a nicer guy. He was carted off to hospital and the police began their investigation and took statements from all 8 of us. To my surprise some six years later myself and one other was summoned back to court in Strabane as the 'victim' was trying to sue the army for £10,000 compensation. Of the 8 soldiers involved that day they could only find two of us, we never ended up giving our evidence but we enjoyed an overnight trip back to Northern Ireland and revisiting Strabane

Later that year the battalion were to be dealt a bitter blow on more than one occasion. On the 8th November 1991 on a windy and rainy day two members of the Close Observation Platoon were tragically killed in a car crash in Armagh whilst on covert operations on their way to Belfast. The vehicle hit a motorway bridge causing the two fatalities and seriously injuring the other two occupants from the same unit. On the morning of the 14th November 1991 I vividly recall being in the corridor of the accommodation block in Omagh ironing my uniform when one of the Riflemen came running out of his room saying that it had just been on the news that an army helicopter had crashed in the Gortin Glen 8 miles north of Omagh. Knowing that it would involve patrols from the battalion I went straight to the Ops room but was told to go away and await further updates. Later that day the whole battalion were instructed to muster at the gym at 1400hrs. I turned up there and joined hundreds of other people, including wives, children and other soldiers from the battalion. The battalion second-in-command stepped up to the floor and I remember to this day the words he spoke: 'It is with profound regret that I announce the death of Cpl Bob Maddocks in a helicopter crash in the Gortin Glen this morning'. This was a tragic blow to the battalion. It transpired that a Lynx helicopter carrying Bob's section plus two pilots had taken evasive action after hitting a flock of birds. Nine others were injured including two seriously. We all left the gym somewhat dumbstruck; there were wives, children and grown men crying. The IRA later tried to claim that they had shot the helicopter down but that was soon ruled out. As if it could not get any worse, a Corporal from HQ Company committed suicide in the guardroom at Omagh only three weeks later. This brought the death toll to four in just less than 4 weeks.

4

The Regiment deploys

Over many decades tourists, visitors and many organised events and visits, as well as everyday commuters, joggers and people going about their normal business would pass by the impressive landmark of Buckingham Palace. Nearby and just around the corner sits the smaller, but even greater tourist attraction of St James' Palace, both of which are within a stone's throw from Clarence House and Horseguards Parade. The monumental gravel-covered parade ground plays host to the Queen's Birthday Parade every year, The Trooping of the Colour, held on the second Saturday of June. At all of these locations can be seen the world-famous Guardsmen stood proudly wearing the distinctive red tunic and bearskin. On Horse Guards Parade on that memorable day hundreds of similarly-dressed soldiers will pound the parade ground performing an immensely impressive military display of precision drill and discipline.

Only a couple of hundred yards from Buckingham Palace and Horse Guards Parade is Wellington Barracks, a more modern-looking barracks set in the centre of London. People going about their normal business would walk past the front gates to be confronted by a soldier in combat dress, wearing a sandy-coloured Guards Regiment beret and armed with a SA80 assault rifle. These two differently dressed soldiers form the same regiment – the unique Coldstream Guards. Their role was two-fold – to defend and protect the monarchy whilst conducting ceremonial duties and to conduct operational commitments in theatres of war worldwide and in particular the conflict in Northern Ireland. Both infantry battalions' personnel are trained and practised to fight against the enemy in a variety of situations in conventional warfare and counter-terrorism. One of the main roles is that of counter-revolutionary warfare, which involved the deployment to Northern Ireland to assist the Royal Ulster Constabulary in the fight against terrorism and more directly to kill or capture terrorists.

Simon initially served in the 1st Battalion Coldstream Guards from February 1986 until October 1990 when he transferred to the 2nd Battalion with fourteen others, their transfer being at a time of great change in both battalions. The 1st Battalion was preparing its move from Wellington Barracks to Munster in Germany, and for its role as the Warrior battalion in the armoured infantry role. This was a role that was considerably different from common infantry skills as a foot soldier, walking long distances with heavy equipment and being expected to remain self-contained for several days at time. A Warrior armoured personnel carrier would be your transport over many miles carrying a section of eight infantry soldiers along with all its equipment. Soldiers had to endure the discomfort of cramped conditions of eight soldiers in a confined space during an uncomfortable ride, and when the 30mm RARDEN cannon would fire, it would rattle a deafening noise throughout the vehicle. And then if the air-conditioning failed in the summer you would then have to endure extremely uncomfortable hot and sweaty conditions, and if the Warrior broke down you could always revert to good old traditional infantry skills – get your kit on your back and walk.

Whilst the 2nd Battalion prepared for its tour of South Armagh from Chelsea Barracks, there was an amount of frantic transfers between the two battalions for those who preferred Germany to UK and vice versa, each for their own reasons. Simon and Rob, a mate of Simon's from the 1st Battalion, both joined 14 Platoon, Number 4 Company 2nd Battalion Coldstream Guards in October 1990.

Simon's new platoon sergeant was Chris P, who was immediately impressed with Simon's arrival in the platoon and commented positively, "He was keen, smart, willing and enthusiastic," which according to Chris was all the qualities of an NCO in the Guards. Simon settled in quickly and despite him being small in stature, or being vertically challenged, he was every inch a guardsman. Rob Baxter remembers the day he arrived following his transfer – "I remember the first day Simon joined the Platoon after his promotion to Lance Corporal. Simon had all his possessions in a heavy box which he dragged up to the second floor of Chelsea barracks by himself; Sweating as he came in through the door he said 'alright lads' with a smile on his face. He never did ask anyone to do something he wouldn't do, unlike some of the others."

The organisation for battle (ORBAT) for each platoon was the responsibility of the platoon sergeant and platoon commander, who had to organise the three sections within the platoon to ensure that each section had the right amount of each rank, equipment and firepower carried. In early January 1991 Chris began this task and realised that the platoon was overstaffed by one Lance Corporal, as only six team commanders were required. One of them would be disappointed, which meant that the seventh NCO would have to undertake the role of a guardsman – it would not be difficult to decide. Typical of the army, it was decided on the good old seniority rule. Unfortunately for Simon he was the junior of them and completed the tour doing the role of a guardsman rather than a team commander, though he still kept his rank. Chris had to tell him and broke the news to him, Simon was not put off by it. Being one of the senior guardsmen in the team Simon volunteered to carry the General Purpose Machine Gun (GPMG), and perform the task of the gunner. This is a heavy machine gun weighing about 15kgs complete with a belt of 200 rounds of 7.62mm ammunition and also carrying an extra 200 rounds of ammunition.

On the contrary, Simon even volunteered to carry the GPMG and perform the role as the gunner in his team. "Are you mad?" was the reply from Chris. "No sarge, I like the weapon and prefer it to the SA80 (rifle)." So, Simon the gunner was born.

Simon was willing to take part in conversations not only with the guardsmen and his peers, but also his seniors and he could hold his own in any debate or joke, with some of the conversation being about his pending marriage during his pre-Northern Ireland leave.

Simon was due to marry Carol on the 9th March 1991 and if he had remained in the 1st Battalion he would have been posted to Munster in Germany, which would have messed up his wedding plans – a second tour of Northern Ireland attracted his transfer too. No sooner had he transferred to the 2nd Battalion than the situation in the Gulf developed and the 1st Battalion was earmarked to deploy there. Simon was keen to complete the tour in Northern Ireland and then return to the 1st Battalion for deployment to the Gulf but he couldn't have his cake and eat it and remained in Northern Ireland.

Not long after Simon and the other transferees settled into the new Company then Northern Ireland training began. This consisted of 'in barracks' training and days spent on Pirbright ranges and rural training areas practicing patrol skills. It was an interesting and realistic package conducted over 2-3 months and run and advised by the Northern Ireland

Simon and his GPMG, the weapon of his choice – both were inseparable from each other.

Training and Advisory Team. The beginning of the training was conducted within the battalion and culminated a month before the tour with some weeks in Stanford Training area, Norfolk and Lyde and Hythe shooting ranges near Folkestone in Kent conducting realistic live firing, rural and urban patrol techniques and scenarios to prepare soldiers for Northern Ireland and for the practice of rural tactics. This was simple. All you had to do was to use an army training area to simulate the fields and hedgerows of rural Northern Ireland. For the urban environment there was a purpose-built village, known as Rype Village, which used to be army married quarters, at Lydd and Hythe in Kent, consisting of houses, shops, streets and a security force base to operate from. Soldiers from a different regiment would perform the role of the civilian population and would be given set scenarios for the guardsmen to deal with.

One of the roles of the company meant that they were expected to be able to patrol self-sufficiently for several days at a time. So most of the training usually involved carrying excessive weight for long periods of time, to get used to carrying Bergens with overnight kit and enough spare batteries, food, water and specialist equipment for up to five days.

The battalion deployed to South Armagh on Monday 11th March 1991. taking over from 45 Commando Royal Marines and began the routine of the tour. For the next six months they were known as the Armagh Roulement Battalion (ARB) and operated in South Armagh, the true staunch Republican area widely known as 'Bandit Country'. This is an area feared by many and over the years has been the killing ground and graveyard of hundreds of victims. Number 4 Company, the Operations Company, known as the 'Ops Company' for short and commanded by Christopher, the OC, was based at Bessbrook Mill. The company's role was to cover the ARB's Area of Responsibility (AOR), provide the Airborne Reaction Force (ARF), and conduct planned operations and other high profile patrolling of their AOR. Chris P and Simon regularly compared tours of South Armagh and Belfast and compared the urban and rural environments. They were both surprised that the terrorists who were operating in Belfast in 1982, when Chris was on his tour, were the same ones that were operating in 1988 when Simon was there.

The company consisted of three platoons and a company headquarters, which consisted of the Company Commander, Company Sergeant Major, company stores and other departments that kept the company operationally effective. The signals detachment made sure all radios and electronic counter-measure equipment was functioning correctly and the Company Sergeant Major ensured that rations and ammunition were available. This left the company quartermaster sergeant responsible for all equipment and vehicles to be operationally effective, which in all was a lot to maintain as there were three operational platoons.

Each company was allocated a lettered prefix call sign to identify them on the radio; Number 4 Company's was Yankee. Fourteen platoon was split into two independent patrol multiples with equal amounts of troops. Because 14 Platoon was the first in the company it was allocated the numbered call sign prefix One Zero. One multiple was commanded by the platoon commander and was known as the Alpha multiple, the other was conducted by the platoon sergeant and was known as the Bravo multiple. Simon was in the platoon sergeant's multiple, known as Yankee One Zero Bravo.

There were three other operational companies deployed throughout the AOR each with specific roles. Number One company was based at Newtownhamilton, Number

Two Company at Forkhill, Number Three Company at Crossmaglen and Battalion Headquarters based at Bessbrook with Number 4 (Ops Company).

The tour progressed over the months with many a varied incident for both multiples, and of course the other companies, to deal with. Rob S was based at Newtownhamilton as the Signals Detachment Commander attached to Number One Company. Rob's job was to ensure that the company radios and other communications equipment was in working order. He was to ensure that all batteries were continually fully charged, the correct frequencies were in use and also to make sure that other electrical items of operational equipment were operational, a very responsible task. "Up until August the tour had been bog standard with not a lot of incidents, and as keen young soldiers almost everyone was waiting for something to happen, to get away from the mundane tour of duty". It was hoped that a goal would be scored for the good guys and maybe have the opportunity to take out some of the enemy. There seemed to be a lot happening around them but not much directed at them. This was probably due to the very high standards of the patrolling that the Ops Company achieved in denying the enemy opportunities to succeed.

Number 4 Company was located at the top floor of an old cotton mill in the small town of Bessbrook, close to the border town of Newry in the staunchly republican area of 'Bandit Country'. Although Simon had only been with the company for five months, his arrival was nothing more than positive. His Company Commander described him to me as a first-class soldier. Even 'Ralphies' positive comments were "I will always think back to how chirpy he was with his smile from ear to ear. He always tried so hard even though he was small in height his stature was twice the man, always determined to do

The Platoon on the heli-pad at Bessbrook Mill. Simon is the left man in the rear rank.

well regardless of the problems that faced him". A previous platoon sergeant from the 1st Battalion commented on his promotion to Lance Corporal, "He was then looking towards his next promotion and intended to go to the Guards depot to train recruits." Simon was so keen and always weaving about the place on some kind of mission or other, so that he acquired the nickname 'Weaver', and everybody had a story about Weaver. Rob S was one of those who transferred from the 1st Battalion and they knew each other well, along with a few of the other transferees so there was a foundation for them to slag off members of the 2nd Battalion, who always wound them up about being ex-1st Battalion. Rob commented, "as normal Simon was in good spirits and always looking forward to going out on patrol". Most of the Company were looking forward to getting home as the tour was the longest the battalion had been on for some time. Johno told me that Simon was full of "you just know…" quotes. Unfortunately one of them was to come true. After one particular crap day, Simon made the comment "you just know that if anyone's going to get wasted on this tour, it's gonna be me; just my fucking luck that'd be". Needless to say that comment remains etched in Johno's memory.

Simon continued to be keen and enthusiastic and his attitude made it easy for him to settle in and get on with people. Dave N was one of them, and was part of the same team as Simon. Dave and Simon were as thick as thieves, both Londoners and both Arsenal fans. Simon was a cheerful individual and would not shy away from a bit of barrack room banter and practical jokes, being the joker himself or on the receiving end. All were boyish pranks and he could give as much as he got and he had a tendency of 'biting back', a lot like me really. On one occasion 'Polly' had filled Simon's sleeping bag with foot powder, covering him from head to toe when he got in it. If it was the army issue powder it would have been cheap and not the normal sweet smelling Johnson & Johnson. Simon was able to calmly shake it off and proceed to giving Polly a bed soaking in revenge. Most of the downtime was spent in the room chatting, smoking and drinking brews and you could almost guarantee that every time you walked into a room Simon would be there. They would discuss what music and equipment was needed for a newly formed band; Simon soon latched onto the group and became a bit of a 'roadie'. The band must have been entertaining, but many years down the line await the release of their first single!!!

Jim C retold another encounter with Simon. "I served with Simon and what can I say, what a cracker! I remember him joining the battalion and thought 'who the fuck is this?' he even ran to scoff with his Bergen on. I remember when we climbed Mount Cook in New Zealand and on reaching the snowline at about 17,000 feet he decided to remove his liner from his Bergen and slide down the slope. As he picked up speed he realised he could not stop in time to avoid the 4,000 foot drop, when all we heard the scream of 'somebody stop me!' We did manage to stop him but fuck me it was really close, he got a good kicking for that one." Jim finished off, "all in all Simon was a cracking soldier with a heart like a lion, I saw him take some knock backs and just saw him bounce back up, what a gutsy little fucker he was and I can still see his smile."

Simon once had the misfortune of losing his wedding ring whilst taking a shower but failed to grab it before it fell down the drainpipe. I remember him telling me about it and how worried he was if Carol found out. To this day I don't think he ever told her. Sorry mate, but she was bound to find out sooner or later. He was extremely concerned and rightly so, how do you explain to your wife that you have lost your wedding ring within only months of getting married? Most blokes would have admitted defeat but he received much piss taking, one being the anonymous gift of a book, which would keep him occupied – JRR Tolkien, *The Lord of the Rings*. He wouldn't let it beat him and after many days of searching he finally obtained the blue prints of the waste drainage system of the Bessbrook Mill and found the ring in a u-bend four floors below. He even contemplated leaving the army to take up plumbing. Patience and perseverance paid off in the end, but that wasn't the only thing he lost and later found. As he was the GPMG gunner his ammunition consisted of belts of 200 rounds in link; he managed to lose three rounds and was subsequently disciplined and fined £30 by the OC. The going rate at that time was £10 per lost round. He later found them under his bed, and even made some enquiries about getting his £30 back but to no avail. It was wisely put towards the Army Benevolent Fund with many other army fines, but at least he now had three spare rounds. He soon made sure that he regularly repainted the red tips of his tracer rounds to make it easy to count for the regular ammunition and kit checks.

Simon was one of the rare individuals who were able to cheerfully take the piss out of someone, but left nothing but good humour and goodwill behind him. Many people were victims, but his essential quality was that he was always respectful of rank (and size) and as such didn't seem to rub people up the wrong way. During one of the early patrols the multiple was tasked to observe a border crossing point for terrorist activity. This was a task that required hours of self-discipline and control in a static location observing one small area all night long, come wind and rain. They were flown to Romeo 21, one of the observation towers near the border, where the patrol would commence once darkness fell. The multiple then split into two six-man teams, one commanded by Chris P and the other by Andy J. Both teams deployed separately and after a few hundred metres both patrols met up and after a quick head check the patrol moved off as one towards the crossing point. After a couple of kilometres they encountered an obstacle in the way, several deep drainage ditches. The bridges could not be used through fear of any possible devices so the decision was made to jump the ditches one at a time. As half of the patrol had successfully jumped the four-foot ditch it suddenly dawned on Chris that he had doubts whether or not Simon would complete the jump, with all his kit, the GPMG and his small frame.

The first suggestion was to throw the gun across (unloaded of course) followed by his kit and then him but Simon was not happy with this option as it would make him vulnerable and he felt it was unprofessional, and if the terrorist had opened fire then he would be without his weapon. Despite the weight and difficult terrain of South Armagh, Simon was inseparable from his GPMG. By this time it was about 11:30pm and after much whispering it was decided that Simon would complete the jump in full kit carrying the gun. Chris, Andy J and the rest of the multiple watched through night vision sights in anticipation, on the far bank as Simon prepared to jump. He took some steps back in preparation and began to launch himself at speed into a running jump to clear the ditch. Just before he reached take off speed he lost his footing but still managed to take off. Unfortunately there was not enough momentum to clear the ditch, and like a racehorse in the Grand National at Beechers Brook, crashed into the cold water of the night. The only thing the others could do was to curl up in fits of laughter. Trying to quieten their giggling due to the tactical situation made it worse and the laughter continued.

Simon was retrieved from the water like a kitten rescued from drowning in a pond; himself, kit and gun completely drenched. The patrol task was not due to end until 7am and Simon could not stay wet in the cold night whilst in a static position. Chris tasked several others to wring his wet clothing out and Simon soldiered on and completed the task without complaining, which wasn't easy to do.

Many people have recalled the events leading up to, and the days that followed and each have their own recollection. Johno recalls passing Simon by the guardroom on the afternoon of Thursday 15th August 1991, just before 1pm. He was fully laden with kit and carrying his GPMG making his way to the heli-pad to deploy. He looked a bit glum having had a fight with another NCO only a few days before. Johno asked if he was all right and characteristically, he gave a quick smile and replied, "Yeah, alright mate. I'll come down for a brew when we're in and have a chin wag". Needless to say he never had that brew.

5

'Contact'

It was Thursday morning, the 15th August 1991 and all of call sign Yankee One Zero Bravo had assembled in the briefing room with anticipation before deploying onto the ground for yet another patrol. Final checks had been done by each team commander to ensure that all weapons and ammunition were accounted for and that all radios and ECM equipment was working and that all the spare batteries were serviceable. Personal checks had been done ensuring that individuals' kit, water and rations were packed away and once the seating plan was filled then the patrol briefing began. An intelligence briefing was given by the intelligence officer detailing the activities and intelligence that had occurred in the patrol area recently and certainly in the past 24 hours. Details of known terrorists, their addresses, vehicles and associates were passed so that the patrol knew who frequented the area. A reminder of the terrorists via personal photographic montages was given in order that they knew who they were looking for.

Sammy then got the attention. Dressed in full combats, his face painted with camouflage cream, his webbing secured to his body, his weapon slung around his neck and his radio earpiece in monitoring the radio traffic, he looked at the eleven soldiers in front of him that he was addressing and issued his orders. A detailed description of the ground and weather that was expected over the next three days was given, along with the patrol task, the patrols mission and how he wanted it executing. After the two team commanders had checked their men, they gave Sammy the nod.

At 1300hrs on Thursday 15th August 1991 callsign Yankee One Zero Bravo left their patrol base at Bessbrook Mill and made the routine short foot journey from the accommodation at the top floor of the mill, down past the memorial garden and out of the front gate passing the guardroom on the left, passing the memories of many soldiers whose memorials stand in the garden and who made that oneway journey out of Bessbrook Mill, never to return. It was a hot sunny day and by the time they had walked a few hundred metres down the hill they begun to warm up with the heavy weight they all carried and they had not even left the patrol base. Fully laden with kit they then crossed the road behind the large cover-from-view screens, the large green metal corrugated iron screens 20 feet high that enabled their movements to be shielded from passing people, or more importantly the nosy watchful eye of the terrorist 'dicker' – a spy that watched their movements to see whether patterns were being set. They continued on to where the heli-pad was and it was there that they were greeted by the darkened, camouflaged Wessex helicopter and overwhelmingly drowned out by the huge noise the rotor blades and loud engine gave off. The heat from the exhaust could be felt, as if the hot summer's day was not enough, and the distinctive smell of burnt aviation fuel. Sat watching and waiting for them, were the pilot and co-pilot and as they briefly arrived the door gunner gave the thumbs up. In single file they climbed aboard, occasionally aided by the door gunner, their heavy Bergens sometimes too awkward to throw board. A quick verbal instruction from the door gunner signaled the pilot to take off. The large sliding door

The memorial garden at Bessbrook Mill, South Armagh.

was closed, though not completely, only enough to enable him to do his job as he held the door-mounted GPMG as it pointed out of the door he scanned the highways and hedgerows, looking for danger and protecting the helicopter as it took off. Their journey had begun into the danger of yet another patrol. Bessbrook was the busiest helicopter landing site in Europe with a steady stream of them coming and going transferring troops and equipment all day long.

Consisting of three four-man teams and commanded by the platoon sergeant, the patrol's mission was to dominate an area of South Armagh near to the border town of Newtownhamilton. More specifically they were tasked to conduct random vehicle checkpoints to deter the movement of terrorists and their equipment by dominating the highway. They were also to conduct house checks on predetermined remote farms and properties to ascertain who lived there and if they were used by any undesirables. Their third task was that of overt patrolling to dominate the ground, a patrol that had been conducted many times in the past. Finally they were also tasked with finding a montage of 96 terrorist photographs that had been lost by a patrol only 10 days earlier.

'Sammy' was the patrol commander and commanded the lead team with the other two teams being commanded by Daz B and Andy J. The patrol was self-sufficient and took enough equipment, food, water and supplies to last three days. Items of specialist equipment were carried by selected individuals who were strategically placed in the patrol both to assist in tasks and for collective protection from terrorist attack. Simon was part of Sammy's team and was the third man of four in patrol formation. As well as his normal weapon and personal equipment he was carrying two items of specialist equipment which would have been concealed and in use to save life, including a bulky and heavy item of electronic counter measure that would enable the patrol to react if an attempt by the terrorist was made to try to detonate a radio controlled IED. Behind Simon was Dave N and in front was Dougie, with Sammy taking the lead. Simon's position in the patrol formation was strategic and important as the electrical protection equipment he carried did not interfere with Sammy's radio and its use would benefit and protect the whole multiple.

The patrol's movement was a slow and methodical operation due to the amount of equipment all the individuals had to carry, progress was slow and the momentum would stop and start as the various patrol tasks were conducted, which were short but thorough. It would have been too risky to remain in one location for more than was necessary otherwise it would have offered the terrorist enough time to set up a quick shoot or grenade attack. Then there were tactical breaks in order to get some food down themselves and rest and of course the hills and hedgerows of the countryside took its toll on the pace of the patrol as obstacles such as roads, rivers, fences and hedgerows had to be negotiated in a professional manner without being vulnerable to any possible terrorist attack.

By the time dusk had fallen and last light had passed by at 2200hrs on Friday 16th August, having recce'd and ensured its safety and security, the patrol laid up for the night about one kilometre west of the planned helicopter pick up point, in a secluded area in remote countryside and out of sight of anybody. Their location, unless they had been compromised, was a secret only known to the Ops room. It was there that would be their time to sort out personal admin, feed, clean weapons and get some sleep for the next day. To ensure their safety sentries were deployed in pairs to ensure everyone's protection throughout the night, and to report any activity.

The night passed peacefully and just before first light both sentries began to wake the multiple in the crisp early August morning to prepare for the move off. It was imperative that the patrol woke, packed their kit, making sure all was secure and weapons ready before a quick bite to eat and a warm brew to kick start the following day's tasks. From the lone lie-up position they had occupied throughout the night in the middle of nowhere and away from any chance of being compromised by local inhabitants the patrol prepared for their longest day.

A moment of brief observation of the surrounding rolling countryside was done, prior to final orders from Sammy before the multiple moved off and by 0730hrs Saturday 17th August the patrol left the lie-up position as three individual teams and made its way to the high ground. From this vantage point and dominating the low ground was Carrickovaddy Wood adjacent to Carrickovaddy Road to its right. This was a medium-size plantation about 100m by 150m consisting of very tall and dense conifer trees planted close together and situated near to the Newtown Road mid-way between the Republican towns of Newtownhamilton and Belleek. In the field north of the wood the proposed helicopter pick-up point was overlooked by the town of Newtownhamilton. It would be all too easy to let your guard down and it was essential that the patrol skills were one hundred percent effective. The patrol would not end until after the debrief, having safely arrived back at Bessbrook Mill. Nobody could have expected what was to confront Yankee One Zero Bravo in the next few hundred metres, neither could anything prevent it. For the remainder it would be their longest day.

Carrickovaddy Wood. The route the patrol took to the proposed helicopter pick up point was over this hill on the approach to the wood from the right.

Aerial photo of Carrickovaddy Wood showing the contact point. Carrickovaddy Wood is the smaller of the two with the gap in the middle.

As Sammy observed the wood from the high ground from the south-west he had decided that his team would enter the wood and patrol along a small fire break from the southern central point to its central northern tip. He knew the layout as he had used the wood as a lie-up only a few weeks earlier. Sammy had tasked Daz B to take his team along the outside on the western side paralleling close to the wood and to the left of Sammy's team. In this location was a small stream, which ran between a fence and the western edge five metres from the wood and consisted of open fields rising up to high ground on the left. Paralleling the fence and stream line adjacent to the wood, Daz's team covered the ground in diamond formation dominating the open ground to the high feature to his left. He was out of sight of Sammy and Andy's teams as they entered the wood but still in radio contact. Sammy had instructed Andy's team to follow him along the track maintaining a tactical safe distance. The track was more of a single vehicle track wide enough for one vehicle.

About 40 metres along the track it branched right then immediately left and then continued through the middle of the wood and by the time you exited the bend the end of the wood was in sight. All four of Sammy's team had negotiated the left bend as he could see all of them behind him as he turned to check the patrol. He had no faults as the team was spread out 3-5 metres apart on opposite sides of the firebreak and alert. By this time they were about 40 metres into the wood. Sammy was walking on a grass mound in the centre of the track, each side of which was the ruts of a vehicle track. The wood was thick and mature in the middle of summer with very tall fern trees and a slight raised embankment on both sides. On the right the wood sloped up with the embankment being slightly higher about 3-4 feet, and to the left it sloped down towards the small stream in the vicinity of where Daz's team were patrolling. It was precisely 08:00hrs and by this time Sammy was about to execute his final tactical manoeuvre in an effort to approach and secure the helicopter pick up that was due in twenty minutes. Sammy intended to branch off the track to the right through the wood to make an appreciation of how the multiple should approach and secure the pick up point from the cover of the trees. By this time Yankee One Zero Bravo were fifty metres into the wood. The early morning summer sun was warming up Carrickovaddy Wood and the dense population of deep

25 02 2003

The track and chicane through the wood. Where the track disappears to the left is where the explosion occurred.

grown coniferous pine trees, lightly misted and damp with mild dew, provided a haven covered from view.

The multiple continued its route and as Dave was the fourth member of the team, he followed a tactical 5 metres behind Simon. As Dave exited the left bend he was faced with a huge bright orange ball, an immense blinding flash and instant heat. The force of the following blast then blew him off his feet knocking him uncontrollably to the ground. He was then bombarded with debris, foliage and rubble as it begun to fall around him and the team, and mayhem and confusion rained, their hearts beating like thunder. Now placed in an evil position of vulnerability they took control of their own protection, to prevent further injuries to themselves, and after a short time they looked for Simon. Faced with adrenalin and fear they faced uncertainty – Simon was not responding to their panicked cries as their eyes scanned the wood, he could not be seen.

The force of the detonation had uprooted a number of huge conifer trees and others were snapped in two as if they were a matchstick. After taking cover for protection from further explosions he got to his feet after some seconds but there was no sign of Simon. Dave then turned around and ran back along the firebreak from where he had come, towards Andy's team. He had been caught in the middle of the explosion and cut off from the rest of his team and realised his only safe option was to backtrack the way he had come. Sammy's immediate observations then saw Dougie stood at the edge of an area of disrupted earth where there had been an explosion, creating a massive crater large enough for a person to stand in. Earth had erupted everywhere dislodging and throwing trees, debris and large boulders into the wood and destroying the track. Sammy and Dougie then ran towards the area of the crater to where Simon would have been but there was no trace of him.

Andy's team was following Sammy's at a safe distance along the track and from his view he watched Simon pass around to the right through a small chicane in the wood, the same feature Sammy and Dave described as the bend. Andy observed Dave follow and out of view, suddenly there was an almighty bang – from Andy's description, more of a 'ka poom', a muffled but hugely loud and massive explosion. The maximum effect was softened by the dense trees which reduced more serious casualties and possibly fatalities. Although out of sight he saw in front of him a huge amount of earth flying from right to left, with soil, debris and grey dust all around landing at his feet. Andy hit the deck, cocked his weapon to put a round up the chamber in the event that he may have to return fire, the immediate action following a contact, and for what seemed like an eternity thought "what the fuck was that?" It was obvious what it was, but nevertheless it was an immediate thought. Pausing for some seconds and not knowing whether it was best to go forward or back his heartbeat pounded faster and faster as he made an appreciation of his immediate action.

Andy was out of direct sight of the contact point and made his way forward cautiously to the bend but could not see around it, for once it was defined, now unrecognisable from destruction. Fallen, uprooted and broken trees obstructed the area along with earth, boulders and debris scattering the track, and by the time Andy reached the area to assist, the track was not so obvious. Unsure of whether to go forward or back, he decided to move forward and at this point saw Dave running towards him. Andy went to the focal point of the explosion and saw the massive crater and destruction for himself. Dave was in shock, as was everyone else and Sammy then decided to withdraw along the way they had

The crater showing the enormous size of the explosion. Nearby trees are destroyed in the blast.

The force of the blast had a more damaging effect.

come. It was right to assume that this route would be safe as they had covered the ground and were not aware of what may lie ahead. They needed to get out of the wood quickly as they were vulnerable. Sammy met up with Andy at the bend in the track only 10 metres back and he told him what had happened and coupled with his own experience Andy then sent an initial contact report to the company ops room. That fateful and dreadful message had been passed to the Ops Room informing them that the multiple had come under a terrorist attack by means of an explosion. This was a message that forced a reaction of support actions, to assist in the immediate follow up in response to Yankee One Zero Bravo's attack and in fact, their rendezvous with the enemy.

Sammy, along with others, returned the few yards to the crater and immediate area to continue the search for Simon. Within the wood confusion, shock and uncertainty still reigned. There was hope that Simon may have been knocked unconscious and out of sight, or that he was delirious and wandered off into the wood but this grew slim. They called for him but no reply, again and again in the hope that he would answer; their fateful cries for help were ignored. Sammy then began to discover pieces of equipment and clothing and he knew at this point that they were not going to find Simon alive. The shock and reality of them realising that a man had been killed began to sink in, but they still felt fearful of a possible secondary attack. They were still alone, with one man down, support had not yet arrived and they remained vulnerable.

Moments later Sammy was joined by Andy and Dougie, and they knew by this time that Simon had been killed in the explosion. Fearing the worse, Sammy decided to move out of the wood and move in again on a back bearing towards the crater to look for Simon. Andy knew that common sense was telling them not just to look left and right, but also up in the trees and that someone was going to find something that they did not want to see. There was no obvious body or any large part, only small pieces of equipment. They continued to call for Simon in the hope that he was missing or was off on the other side of the wood, but he was never going to answer them. They then began to find what Andy describes as small amounts of brightly coloured pink combat material on a number of trees near the crater and after a short time it began to sink in that there was a certainty that Simon had been taken out by the explosion and that they would not find him. They were right.

Sammy then ordered the patrol out of the wood through fear of the possibility of a secondary device, or further terrorist attack, and then instructed them to set up vehicle

Looking towards where Simon approached the contact point.

checkpoints and cordon points on the Carrickovaddy Road, to secure the area and the remote possibility of catching any fleeing terrorist. There was never a chance of the latter as the terrorists would only attack if they knew their escape route was clear. The risk of protection from a secondary device was outweighed by the urgent need to establish what happened to Simon. Even after a sixty minute search the multiple still had not found anything that provided conclusive proof of Simon's death.

So large was the explosion that the commanding officer heard it from his office at Bessbrook Mill some 15 miles from the scene and a patrol from the Reconnaissance Platoon who were operating an observation post six miles away on the border experienced their shelter rocked by the force of the explosion. One of the commanders at that OP recalls, "When the booby trap was tripped the roof of our OP actually shook with the shock wave, we were at least 10km (6 miles) away. Immediately there was pandemonium on the radio net with the company commander trying to get a grip of the situation and to ascertain what had actually happened." Although Yankee One Zero Bravo were based at Bessbrook, on this specific patrol they were operating in the Newtownhamilton area, for which Number 2 Company was responsible.

Shortly before 0800hrs on Saturday 17 August the duty signaler, Lee, who was the signals detachment commander for Number 2 Company, was in the process of taking over from the night signaler in the Ops room at Newtownhamilton as the radio operator for the day. Lee took over in the normal manner and was briefed by the off-coming radio operator. Lee knew that Yankee One Zero Bravo were operating in the area and were soon to get picked up. Next to the ops room was the intelligence cell and a hatch opening through to the ops room for communication. Also on duty with Lee were a senior NCO and a CCTV operator and as a team they ran the Ops room during their tour of duty monitoring all patrol and helicopter movement. Lee popped into the intelligence cell for a cigarette to kick start his day, in earshot of the radio. After about three puffs

The track which would have led the patrol to the helicopter pick-up point.

on his cigarette he heard those fateful words "CONTACT EXPLOSION IN AREA OF NEWTOWNHAMILTON, WAIT OUT!!!" – the normal brief initial report after contact with the enemy.

The cigarette was quickly extinguished and he rushed into the ops room to take up his position on the net (radio) to initially coordinate procedures. Soon after, he began to receive radio reports from the patrol commander that there had been an explosion and a location was given and Lee knew that it was the ops company patrol. It wasn't long before every man and his dog began to fill the ops room. The company commander, Stephen, then took control of the radio and began to command and coordinate the follow up. Lee then began to log everything that was said and done as further reports were coming in from the patrol on the ground. They weren't good and panic and controlled aggression set in. Staff in the ops room could not imagine the scene of the explosion and were not aware of what they were doing at the scene.

At 08:06hrs a Rat Trap was called by the Battalion Ops room in the Newtownhamilton area, deploying ground troops to secure main roads and conduct vehicle checkpoints in the hope of cutting off any possible fleeing terrorists. They weren't to know at this time that they would never catch anyone in the immediate follow up, but it was standard operational procedures that had to be done. At 08:09hrs Sammy began to report that he had done a head count and was missing a member of the patrol, with a possible casualty in the wood. He continued to report having repeatedly searched the area and all that could be found were bits of Bergen and equipment. Lee recalls that the patrol commander was in a bad way, shock had set in and he didn't realise he had lost a man. The watch keeper, a senior NCO manning the radio, had told Sammy over the radio to "get his men in three ranks and physically count them". There is some substance to that story, but I find it harsh for somebody in a secure environment some miles from the scene of an explosion, where soldiers had witnessed the murder of a colleague to dictate on the radio, belittling a commander to count his men when he was in an expected state of shock and was sure one was dead, having witnessed a murder of a mate and no doubt feeling responsible. As the morning went on, it became apparent that Simon had been killed in the explosion.

More people began to visit and loiter around the ops room and word soon spread throughout the company location at Newtownhamilton and other locations throughout the battalion's area. Everyone was anxious to know what was happening. Everyone wanted to get out and help but there was anger and hatred in the air. More patrols began to be deployed and by now it had become a serious incident.

At 08:12hrs the fire brigade attended the scene and from the army's point of view there wasn't much they could do. Arriving twelve minutes after the explosion they were met by eleven soldiers running around trying to get to grips with what they should be doing, more importantly trying to locate a possible casualty or by now a fatality in the wood. Not even a body had been found which made it even more frustrating. But the fire brigade had a job to do as well as Sammy's multiple, as there had been a report of an explosion they had to attend to deal with any further danger.

Micky L was the commander of the Airborne Reaction Force 'top cover' and their job that morning was to provide airborne cover while the helicopter completed the extraction of Yankee One Zero Bravo. The helicopter was just in the process of lifting off the heli-pad at Bessbrook when the contact report was transmitted over the radio. Mick then shouted to his troops to be quiet so that he could initially monitor the radio but it was difficult enough to hear yourself think over the sound of the rotor blades. He then told his troops that Yankee One Zero Bravo had been contacted and that they were going to the scene. The lads became very anxious as nobody knew what they were going into and Mick recalls there was a lot of activity on the radio. Sammy was heard to be sending constant SITREPS to update the Ops room, and the Ops room was desperately trying to find out if there was a casualty.

Mick's team continued the flight to the Newtownhamilton area, only a matter of minutes, and had heard that one of them was missing. The missing soldier's personal identification number, used in case of casualty identification, enabled Mick to rapidly realise that it was Simon. By this time it was 08:14hrs, fourteen minutes after the explosion and Mick's ARF team had just been deployed on the ground. Mick described the manner of which his troops performed as "professional mode straight away" and he continued to describe the situation as "very hard". Mick was angry and was in tears, but he was not the only one, and being a Christian he initially felt angry with God because of what had happened and he could not understand why it had happened. But that is life, a life that in times of war is a life of risks, a life of facing threats and life-depending times. Times and chances in Northern Ireland that are taken. By this time there was not a lot more that could have been done in the immediate follow up.

At 08:40hrs call-sign Echo One Zero Alpha (the platoon commander of 14 platoon), Echo Two Zero Alpha (the platoon commander of 15 platoon), Echo Two Zero Bravo (the platoon sergeant of 15 platoon) and Echo Zero Alpha (the Company Commander), had deployed to the scene and along with Mick's ARF team had begun to set up cordon positions around the contact site and began to take control of the situation ready for the deployment of other agencies to gather evidence to assist the police investigation. Mick noticed that the remainder of Sammy's multiple were in a very bad way and at 09:30hrs Yankee One Zero Bravo were extracted from the area 300m south west of the contact point back to Bessbrook Mill.

6

A nod of the head from John

The platoon commander's multiple, Yankee One Zero Alpha, also deployed on a three day patrol on the same day as Yankee One Zero Bravo. Though working independently from Yankee One Zero Bravo, their patrol tasks were similar but their operation had concentrated on a nearby patrol route, not too far from Yankee One Zero Bravo but close to the South Armagh border. Just before 8am on Saturday 17th August 1991 the platoon commander's multiple was extracted from the ground in the area of Newtownhamilton first and returned to Bessbrook. They had been the last to deploy on the Thursday from Bessbrook Mill and were the first to be picked up, having patrolled a similar area, and their helicopter extraction plan was the same time as Yankee One Zero Bravo. It doesn't sound much, but when you are in that situation it's surprising how much it boosts your morale to 'be back before the rest of the platoon'.

Having been safely flown back to Bessbrook Mill they left the heli-pad and returned to their accommodation to clean their weapons, sort their kit and replenish radio and ECM batteries and other equipment and generally sort themselves out, and once that was done then they would look forward to some rest. Army routine was drummed into each soldier that on return from an operational patrol, you would sort out your weapon, equipment, replenish water and rations and batteries before you shower or sort yourself out. This was in case an immediate redeployment was needed, and following this incident, it was the case. This routine had been done time and time before. The platoon commander still fully kitted up, made his way straight to the Ops Room to report that they were all back safe and well before compiling his patrol report. His patrol report took about an hour or so to complete before he submitted it to the intelligence unit for analysis and intelligence gathering to be used to target future tasking. From here the platoon commander's routine was different from what the rest of the multiple was doing, but events were to take a dramatic change.

No sooner had the troops set foot through the door of the accommodation than the platoon commander burst in from the other end in a bit of a flap. He told the multiple: "There's been an explosion at Newtownhamilton and Corporal Ware is missing." Immediately almost everyone chorused "What the fuck are they doing in Newtownhamilton? We've just left them near Carrickovaddy Wood!" The commanders amongst them switched on their radios and everyone listened attentively and within minutes it was all horribly clear and they remained in the room fully kitted up for about half an hour waiting for an immediate redeployment. Minutes seemed like hours and eventually the platoon commander returned and closed the door behind him. Despite his face being still covered in camouflage cream and sweating, he was white as a ghost. He was trying to say something but his words were mumbled as shock had set in, pausing for a few seconds he then came out with it, "Basically Corporal Ware's fucking well dead." A stunned silence was followed by frantic questions and theories as to what had happened. There was clearly no time to drag this one out as to what had happened as it was now more important to be in a position to quickly redeploy to the contact area to assist and support the troops on the ground.

An hour later the platoon commander's multiple were ready to deploy back to the scene to assist in the cordon and the follow up, at about the same time as Simon's multiple returned to the Bessbrook Mill. As Yankee One Zero Bravo walked back to their rooms they did so in complete silence, no tears, and no angry comments just a grim distant look about them.

Bri was in 15 platoon, 4 Company and returned from a night patrol in the early morning of Saturday 17th August. He was in his room when news filtered down that there had been an explosion involving members of the company. Like many commanders in a similar position that morning, he turned on his radio to monitor events unfolding to find a tense frustrating and frantic time and at first the information was sketchy, as it always was in those situations – a lot was going on behind the scenes but not much was filtering through. The Mill became a hive of activity with the ARF being deployed and troops running all over to pass and receive information and trying to confirm or dispel any rumours. It soon became clear that there had been an explosion south of Newtownhamilton in a wooded area close to the border, and there were some casualties. The rest of the time was spent listening to events unfold and trying to realise what had happened. When word got through that there had been a fatality all sorts of things were going through Bri's mind, mainly who had been killed, but more concerned that it had happened anyway. The fact remained that the terrorists had got someone So near to the end of the tour, a time that was very vulnerable, and as a result of this the battalion was gutted.

Elsewhere in the battalion Area of Responsibility Woody began his stint on 'stag' in the observation tower of Golf 40 as he climbed the steps to the top of the sangar just a few minutes before 8 am.

> I closed the door to the sangar at exactly the same time that the bomb went off a few kilometers away and thought that it was a big one. The radio crackled into life and I heard the contact report being sent. The second radio was switched on to the Newtownhamilton channel so that events could be monitored. We heard that there had been a landmine and that Cpl Ware could not be found. I stood there and listened to the radio as they tried hard to deal with the explosion, and I recalled the instructions over the radio – "…..look in the trees" but the response was harsh "….. we can't find him, we can't find him anywhere.
>
> I sat there wondering Why they could not find a body. More reports were heard that they had found some GPMG ammunition and a first field dressing. I could hear the emotion in the voices and I was expecting them to find him at any moment, but for an hour it did not happen, and as time progressed it transpired that Simon would never be found. It was very uncomfortable sitting there listening to what was going on.

Mark R was on duty in the Buzzard Ops room at Bessbrook Mill, the Ops room which controls the helicopter flights in and out of Bessbrook Mill. Shortly after 8am a Wessex helicopter was preparing to take an under-slung load to Newtownhamilton for a resupply and a second Lynx helicopter was flying 'top cover' in support, to prevent any possible terrorist attack. The Wessex was 'wound up' with its rotors going and ready to lift from Spot 4 with 6 members of the ARF. In the front of the Ops room the skids of the Lynx were lifting and the Wessex was in the hover ready to have its load connected when the intercom tannoy from the battalion Ops room echoed… "Contact area of Newtownhamilton, Contact area of Newtownhamilton". Mark relayed the report to both helicopter pilots over the radio and the Lynx helicopter immediately left and flew to the contact area to provide support. Rob S was the passenger in that Lynx. "I don't know whether the contact happened while I was waiting or just as we were taking off, but when we were in the air the door gunner told me there had been a contact just outside of Newtownhamilton and that we were going to fly over the area to provide 'top cover.' There was only the pilot, co-pilot, door gunner and Rob on board so they were not capable of being deployed on the ground. It was only a matter of minutes before they were on the scene and began to circle about 200m above the contact site. Rob was given a pair of headphones and was shown an area to observe by the door gunner. Rob observed a wooded area with a track and a huge hole like something you would expect on the moon. "The worst of it all was the colours that I saw, the track was brownish, the hole was yellow but around the tree tops was pinky-green". Naively Rob asked the door gunner why the trees were a pinky colour and was met with the reply "What do you think?" The Lynx remained airborne for a while and all Rob could do was to monitor the radio and observe the devastation, but could not bring himself to look away. Rob was thinking all the time, "poor bastard, I hope he wasn't anyone I know" At the time Rob had no idea who the patrol belonged to. The Lynx continued to Newtownhamilton and Rob went immediately to the Ops room to get more information. "It wasn't long before I found out it was Simon and all I could think was … Oh Fuck."

The Wessex at Bessbrook was disconnected from its load, landed and awaited the arrival of the six remaining ARF crew. They soon arrived and the helicopter lifted and then flew to the contact site. Mark remained in the Buzzard Ops room and after some hours the Wessex returned with the rest of Simon's patrol. The drone of the rotor blades could be heard as the helicopter approached the Mill, as it flew low on its approach the grey image of the heavily-laden Wessex appeared as it headed towards the landing site. The helicopter, being just within its load limit, had returned the eleven members in one lift and the pilot gave a clear warning to the ops room of his emergency approach and the heli-pad was cleared so that the Wessex could make a rolling land, as it would not be able to hold the hover. The helicopter just made it over the back fence having a bit of a bumpy landing and rolled along three of the landing spots and safely to a stop.

Rob M had been part of the platoon commander's multiple, but due to a knee injury he had not gone on the patrol that day. On the morning of the 17th August he had dismounted guard at Bessbrook and was on his way back to his room when he heard there had been an explosion. He turned on his radio and having missed the initial contact report, heard many situation reports and frantic messages which did not sound good. He knew that there had been a casualty and quickly became aware from the call sign that it was his platoon. Originally Rob had heard the NIPIN, Whiskey 3163, transmitted over the radio as the casualty and could not immediately put a name to it. In stunned disbelief it was confirmed when his name was sent in full some time later. Everyone is allocated an identification number to assist in casualty identification, known as the Northern Ireland Personal Identification Number, NIPIN for short, and it was the first letter of your surname followed by your last four figures of your regimental number.

Sam was a platoon sergeant in 15 platoon, 4 Company and remembers the morning vividly. "My multiple were asleep at the Mill when the sound of the explosion woke me right on 8am. Out of instinct I got up and roused the troops anticipating a deployment and once the situation had been established the whole company was stood to."

Andy P was a member of the anti-tank platoon who were due back out on patrol before first light. "Probably an hour or two after returning from a night-time patrol we were woken by an almighty thud! and we knew what it was straight away, so we had our kit ready and were straight back out. We flew over the crater in the woods that the bomb had made, and it made me feel sick because we knew there were casualties, but we didn't know who it was straight away."

Yankee One Zero Bravo were on their way back to Bessbrook and Sam met Simon's multiple as they returned to the heli-pad. As the helicopter came to a stop, the patrol all got off professionally; they retrieved their kit and headed out of the marked danger area of the rotor blades, the immediate action once you exit a chopper. They initially sat on their Bergens and their weapons were handed over to other members of the company to be unloaded. Mark saw that many of them were in tears. A few minutes later, the company second-in-command rounded up some other company members and assisted them to take their kit back to the accommodation as the remainder of the patrol made their way to a debrief area. There, he was tasked to take the troops through supervising the unloading of weapons. It was a common practice for commanders to supervise the unloading of weapons for safety, not just for this incident. Sam recalls that many of the eleven guardsmen were distraught at what had happened, some of whom were openly crying. Once safely back, Sam's multiple deployed with the rest of the company to assist in the operation to the cordon and satellite areas whilst the clearance and search was conducted. Sam's multiple provided protection to the static cordon troops by way of patrolling to the north of the

The mangled remains of Simon's GPMG - all that was found
of the weapon and 400 rounds of ammunition.

wood. Even though they were a kilometre away they could clearly see the wood and the crater left at the scene. It was a very sobering experience.

Lee had heard the news confirming the death and the name Simon Ware. He realised that he didn't know him but it hurt just as much as if it was his best mate, "Because you know it is us and them and the scum had taken one of our boys." The local milkman, who was an IRA sympathiser, associate and possibly had terrorist connections, was seen that day driving around the cordon area laughing. He soon stopped when several troops gave him a bit of a hard time and then emptied every one of his milk bottles. Rob recalls that although everyone knew that Simon had been killed it was not until later that day that it was confirmed that he was dead. After they had heard that his mangled GPMG was found some distance from the contact site they knew for certain. "Morale was low in the company after this tragedy and it was a credit to the leadership in the company that kept the Ops Company in focus with the job in hand".

One of Rob's worst feelings was that his multiple had gone back out to help but there was nothing they could do to assist. One thing that upset him and others later was when two NCOs who had no knowledge of Simon were tasked to pack all his kit into a box. They were detailed to go through the clothes and equipment of the soldier who had died, as they didn't know Simon therefore not causing too much distress for colleagues. Rob ensured that at least his kit was packed with some dignity.

The following account was from the Sergeant of the Close Observation Platoon.

I was serving as the Close Observation Platoon Sergeant during the South Armagh tour when Simon was sadly killed. My platoon had been running an observation post since our arrival on the Slieve Gullion mountain feature overlooking 'Slab Murphy's' new place in the South and I happened to be in the COP ops room at the time of Simon's death. I can clearly remember the contact report from Sammy the patrol commander and it was one of complete shock. I recall him stating that he couldn't locate Simon and that he was digging with his hands in the belief that he was buried.

Garry Thompson was a corporal in The Royal Green Jackets and employed as the signals detachment commander to the author's company. He first met Simon on a parachute course at Netheravon Airfield in Wiltshire in April 1988.

They became friends during the course, and enjoyed a few nights out as the weather wasn't very good for parachuting. During the course Simon mentioned to Garry that his brother was a Royal Green Jacket in 2 RGJ and the two soon formed a friendship and served in the same Company for a while.

I remember the day Simon was killed, I was in the Bn ops room in Omagh when a contact report was sent on the PIN (Province Incident Net) which was monitored by every Ops room in the province. I remember that based on information received, including Simon's unit call sign, I was able to put two and two together and had a very bad feeling it was Simon. I then left the ops room to carry on with my task for the day. I remember going home and watching it on the news that evening and being told the next day about Darren being rushed back to the mainland.

There have been many comments about the morale felt and experienced by individuals who had different involvement in the follow up or who had no involvement at all. Simon's death had a profound affect on the battalion and even the Commanding Officer admitted that it was a massive blow for the battalion. Clearly everyone was saddened, but in many ways his death strengthened their resolve to carry on and to do the job properly and not to lose any professionalism or to underestimate the threat they faced.

One of the strengths that grew over the time in South Armagh was a great deal of friendship with all the troops in the company that was deeply felt when Simon was lost.

Morale was extremely low, lower than it had ever been. Bri went to his room and cried, like many others, and just could not believe what had happened, and many were completely devastated. As the company and the remainder of the battalion deployed on the clearance operation, Bri recalls being sat in a trench on a cordon position over night, and at the time he did not know how Simon had died, or whether his body was still in the wood. All he could remember was being in the trench on that clear summer night with the moon silhouetting Carrickovaddy Wood, as the Company had dug in to secure the area thinking that right behind him in a wood lay the body of a colleague and a good friend. Bri remembers, for the rest of the tour the place was full of sadness but being professional as they all were, they had a job to do. They continued to carry out their task as professionally as they had begun since they arrived and collectively vowed that Simon would be the only one. Bri's recollection of Simon was "a happy go lucky guy, who was a good laugh and kept up morale. He still is definitely missed by me and all members of the battalion who knew him. He certainly will never be forgotten."

Andy J went on to express his own personal thoughts of hearing stories from ex-servicemen from the Second World War. Telling experiences of loosing many friends on a daily basis during the war, feeling sorrow, but still able to continue on and trying to forget. "When we lost Simon the despair and loss felt enormous and amplified maybe because it was one man and not hundreds. I personally thought that losing one man was more devastating than losing a number in an all-out war or conflict. The feelings and despair I felt were amplified and focused in that one horrific event." Andy J continues, "In a conventional war or conflict things may have felt different, but dealing with the terrorist, no matter how much training to counter the terrorist threat was done, there was an enormous amount of gut feeling, like hatred, vengeance, anger, waste and sitting ducks unable to fight back. Thoughts of the incident occurred all the time, even on stag outside a newly-built part of Bessbrook Mill, weeks after where the smell of the cement was the same as the smell of the earth falling around me after the explosion."

Chris B, who was a patrol commander in the anti-tank platoon, Support Company, admitted that Simon's murder would stick in the minds of everyone he knew. Chris B's call sign, Echo Two Zero Bravo, were one of the clearing patrols going through the wood as part of the search operation in the immediate and subsequent follow up that day. "After many hours of following the trace up and down and looking all over the shit hole we moved off and out of the woods, hills and tracks and gave the all clear that nothing else could be found." For the record, he told me that there were no signs of an alarm or anything to indicate what we now know was there.

Chris P, Simon's platoon sergeant when Simon transferred, bade farewell to 14 platoon in mid-May of 1991 when he was posted as an instructor to Sandhurst Military College where he trained officer recruits and was taken over by Sammy. As Chris cleared out his married quarter in London he heard the news on his car radio that a soldier had been killed in South Armagh, but no name or regiment was given. He went straight to Chelsea barracks and spoke to the Families' sergeant, John. He quizzed John at length but knowing that he couldn't tell him, he played the veiled speech game

"Do I know him?"

A nod of the head from John

"Is he Support Company?"

A shake of the head from John

"Is he Four Company?"

A nod of the head from John

This is not good, Chris thought to himself.

"Was he in my platoon?"

A nod of the head from John

God, Chris thought, who could it be? It wasn't long before John dropped the bombshell.

"He hasn't been married long."

"Oh Christ its 'Weaver' Ware isn't it?"

A nod of the head from John.

Chris was devastated, and as he climbed back into his car to drive to Sandhurst his wife turned to him and asked if it was one of his. He replied "Yes".

Don, who was once Simon's platoon sergeant, was also an instructor at Sandhurst when he watched the television when the mid-day news broke of a soldier killed in South Armagh. "I knew immediately it was going to be a Coldstreamer. I then started thinking who I knew in the 2nd Battalion and wondered what are the chances of it being any of the ten men that I knew in that battalion. I even thought it can't be Simon, he is far too young to die." Hours went by before his name was confirmed on the evening news. "When I heard the evening news and Simon was named I was gutted. I was very shocked that out of over 600 men, it had to be the young lad from my platoon before he went to the 2nd Battalion." Don went onto say that Simon was bigger than others. "He always seemed to be happy and very well mannered and the keenest Coldstreamer you would ever wish to know."

Nothing could prepare you for what had started out as such a happy and fun day to have such a tragic and heartbreaking end.

Captain Keith R was the Unit Families' Officer and was responsible for the link between the battalion in Northern Ireland and the wives and children back in England. The following account is a personal one that describes the utmost and hardest task of not only trying to delay any of the wives detecting something was wrong as the ferry sailed to England, but having to break the news on their arrival at Dover.

I, as Families Officer, aided by Sergeant Phil Crouch and Lance Sergeant John Hinds, had organised a day's shopping trip for the Wives Club to Calais. Everyone was on good form, the girls were all in high spirits, excited at the thought of spending hubbies money and doing what girls do best...... shopping with no nagging!" The day started by collecting all the wives from the various pickup points in that 'old household division' stalwart, 'Slim's Bus'. Not the most reliable mode of transport but driven by one of the worlds nicest Grenadiers, Slim (who would play a sterling part later on).

Come mid-afternoon following all the normal duty-free shopping most of the wives had met up for a few drinks prior to returning to the bus and making their way back to the ship. "As the coach was boarding the ferry a member of security discreetly approached me and asked if I was Captain R. Once he ascertained that I was he then asked me to make myself known to a member of the ships' crew once everyone was on board." The wives were totally oblivious as to what was happening and made their way to one of the bars and happily carried on where they had left off in Calais.

In the pit of my stomach I knew there was something wrong, particularly when I was led to the Bridge, introduced to the ship's Captain and then led to his cabin. There he confirmed my fears and via the ship's radio I spoke with the Regimental Adjutant Major Hugh Towler who informed me of the tragic death of Simon. Between us it was agreed that we would not tell Carol or anyone else until we were back in Dover.

For the next forty five minutes he was back and forth to the Captain's cabin arranging with Hugh how and where Carol would be told, all the time returning to the wives sitting directly opposite Carol, listening to her and watching her laugh whilst the rest of the wives happily told stories of their day's adventure and the "billy bargains" they had bought.

Throughout all of this Slim played a blinder, the wise old owl had spotted something awry when they had boarded the boat. "Err Guv, what's the problem?" he asked. I quietly told him what had happened. "Right Guv, you crack on and leave the girls to me, I'll look after them." And being the raconteur that he was he kept an eye on them throughout and remained outstanding throughout.

On arrival at Dover the ship's authorities cleverly and discreetly shepherded the party away from the rest of the passengers and as they approached customs they were met by Hugh Towler and a policewoman. "You could see the look of concern on the wives' faces as Carol was led away to a side room."

Hugh Towler then had the thankless task of telling Carol of the day's awful events, which he did with as much sensitivity as possible. The next five to ten minutes were horrendous; Carol reacted as any wife would after losing her husband of only six weeks."

Carol was then taken home in the staff car by Hugh where family and friends would meet her and the Regimental welfare process began.

In the meantime Slim and Phil Crouch led the rest of the wives back to the bus. "On rejoining the wives on the bus I broke the news to them, their reaction was as one would expect, much wailing and pouring out of grief at the tragic loss of Simon and sympathy for Carol." A tragic day.

On Sunday 18th August the Ops Company gathered in the attic of Bessbrook Mill as the Company Second-in-Command prepared to address the company. The Company Sergeant Major had gathered the company and handed over to the 2i/c, Guy, for his address. As he looked at the men he could tell by the faces that with only a few weeks to go on the tour, they were physically and mentally drained by the tragedy. He then proceeded to address the company:

You all now know of the tragic loss of Cpl Ware whilst on patrol yesterday. You all must be aware that nothing more could have been done by the multiple and Cpl

Ware, who was killed instantly, did not suffer. His wife who was on a trip to France with members of the battalion wives club was informed on her return to the UK where she was met by the Regimental Adjutant.

His brother who was serving with the Royal Green Jackets here was informed yesterday and returned to the UK to be with his family. Cpl Ware's mother was personally visited and informed by Major Cox.

The Brigade Commander commended the multiple on their reaction and actions after the explosion and numerous people have telephoned and asked me to pass on condolences to the Company and a file of messages has been opened.

I will inform everyone as soon as I know of funeral and memorial arrangements. Mrs. Ware has requested a full military funeral, which will probably take place in the Guards Chapel. Yankee One Zero Bravo (complete) and Mr. Barry will attend the funeral and find the 6 bearers.

It is essential that we the company are strong and that we help everyone to get over this tragedy, but it is imperative that our professionalism, appearance and attitude to the public, the enemy and within the battalion is not affected and that we continue to show ourselves as the thoroughly professional company we are.

Cpl Ware, who will be missed by all, would expect nothing less.

As he ended the address he looked up and saw that there was not a dry eye in the attic. The Company Sergeant Major brought the company to attention and dismissed them to their duties.

7

My darkest, lonesome day

In August 1991 I was the second-in-command of my section of eight soldiers. My responsibility lay with the command of a team of four but in the absence of the section commander, then I would take over the reins of the command of the eight man section. The Company was based at a small security force base called Rockwood, situated about three miles south east of the County Tyrone town of Castlederg. This was a small security force base nestled beside the large River Derg and hidden from view by the rural features of natural habitation. Though it was no secret location it had been there for many years and was a hotel in its former life. Apart from the Ops Company we formed part of it was also the home of the local Ulster Defence Regiment Company who used it as a patrol base. Surrounded by large cover-from-view screens and overlooked by tall observation towers, it was the life and soul of the battalion Ops Company. The operations room, intelligence cell and offices were contained separately, as too were the accommodation, rest areas and cookhouse and each building was protected from mortar and bomb attacks by strengthened blast walls. Our company accommodation consisted of several portakabin-type rooms joined together and surrounded by mortar-proof blocks – eight men to a room plus the signals store room at the end of the narrow corridor. There were other rooms within the complex that afforded some comfort in the way of a gym, laundry rooms, showers, the TV room and a shop and all were protected too. I would often forget to realise that I was with my battalion only about 30 miles or so from Simon's battalion and we were doing the same job.

It was 06:30am on Saturday 17th August 1991. The QRF commander, Cpl 'Frank' woke the whole Company quickly as another incident had occurred on our company area. The quiet Saturday morning was now wakened by the assertiveness of troops and commanders rallying around rushing to deploy to yet another terrorist incident. This time a small handheld coffee jar grenade had been thrown at the house of an off-duty UDR soldier in Castlederg, and had failed to detonate. The Mark 15 'coffee jar' grenade as it was known was a fairly new type of device at the time currently being used by PIRA. It was first introduced on 25 May 1991 when a soldier was killed in an explosion within North Howard Street Mill in Belfast when the device was thrown over a wall and detonated inside the security force base. The grenade was based on a design seen in the early 1980's. Up until the end of 1991 seven variants had been identified across Northern Ireland of which at least three had been seen in the Armagh area in a dozen incidents since July of 1991. The components were very simple, consisting of a glass coffee jar, a bell push button plus an amount of explosive and 'scrap yard shrapnel' – a collection of nuts and bolts designed to have the effect of shrapnel when it detonated. There were slight variations to each device and mechanism and it was a common occurrence at that time, as a lot of these Mk15 grenades weren't detonating due to its new construction. It was possibly a bad batch of explosive or the inexperience of the terrorist when being constructed. I suppose it made our lives and the RUC's easier, and of course it didn't harm anyone, but it kept the ATOs busy.

Back at Rockwood the Company was getting dressed and sorting out kit, making sure we had all that was necessary as we did not know how long we would be deployed for, but no doubt most of the day. The company I was in (A Company) was really professional and there was a good bunch of experienced and keen soldiers of all ranks who always got on with the task, and morale was pretty high. Like many incidents before and after, things went smoothly and that reflected in the professionalism of everyone, backed up by the OC having said that he had confidence in us.

Back at Rockwood there was no time for breakfast. Other agencies and police had put a loose cordon around the bomb scene and were waiting the arrival of further troops and the ATO. The semi-detached house was on the left side of the Castlefinn Road, just on the edge of town on the road that leads to the border of Eire, which was only about a mile away. The terrorist may have used that road as an escape route or merely mingled back in the small town as if nothing had happened. Rockwood was about three miles from the bomb scene and was too close for a helicopter deployment meaning that the troops either walked or were dropped off by vehicle. By the time a helicopter was arranged to fly from Omagh, pick up at Rockwood and then drop off outside Castlederg we could have walked it.

We arrived at the scene having been briefed and we received a quick set of orders and I briefly spoke to an RUC officer who didn't have much to say about what had happened and I got on with my section's task. Mark was the section commander and our simple task was to satellite patrol around the inner cordon to provide protection for troops at the scene and to dominate the ground to the east of the cordon. I initially passed the time of day with Dave G briefly on a quiet street on an estate behind the police station. This was a predominantly Protestant estate which was quiet and did not give us any problems. I had earlier been his best man for his very eventful wedding day in February 1991 prior to our deployment to Northern Ireland. Eventful in that it's not every wedding that you turn up two and a half hours late having been cut out of your car by the fire brigade after crashing side-on into a magistrate's car rushing to the church.

We both had the same idea that we were going to have a long day ahead just patrolling until the ATO had made the bomb safe, a task that we were used to. We'd done it before and no doubt we would do it many more times and fortunately it was a dry and sunny day. Unbeknown to me at the time, my day was probably going to be the longest one, a day that will remain clear to me.

I heard over the company radio net a message from the Adjutant to the Company Commander to ring him on the secure telephone. The Adjutant, of all people – why would he want to speak to the OC in the middle of an operation? He was based at Battalion Headquarters in Omagh and would have no involvement in the incident we were dealing with. I pulled a face to myself, as it was unusual for that to be transmitted, particularly in the middle of an incident and miles from battalion headquarters. The company commander had asked if it could wait but was clearly told 'no' and I recall the distinct reply from the Ops officer of "No, it's urgent" The OC then made straight to Castlederg RUC station. Even he admitted to me later that his mind started to race, and he detected something was wrong. The Adjutant told the OC what had happened, and he now had the grim task of telling me, one that he did not look forward to.

Some of us on the clearance operation assumed that there had been another incident, possibly at our other company location at Strabane. A short time passed and the company commander called the platoon sergeant, Martin H, on the radio and said "I need a call sign to assist with another task, you have Foxtrot Two One Delta with you, and I need to use them".

Foxtrot Two One Delta was my call sign and I was told by the company commander to return to Castlederg police station with my team. I walked along the main road, grinning at other troops who would be staying a bit longer on the clearance operation, knowing that I was probably going to get a better and responsible job. But it felt odd that the OC was only using one team, as the minimum to be used was two. It wouldn't be long before that grin was to be wiped off my face.

We arrived at Castlederg police station and were met by the company commander and the CSM, Jamie H. My team and I were ushered into a Land Rover and we made the short journey by road back to Rockwood escorted by the QRF. I asked the OC what the job was, but he insisted he briefed me in his office on return.

The Land Rover came to an abrupt halt outside the company operations room. The OC jumped out first, grabbed me and as he began to lead me up the stairs to the ops room I heard the CSM tell my team in a firm voice to get out and go with him. The CSM later told me, "whilst the OC was giving you the news of your brother's death, I told your team what I knew had happened and told them to pack your kit as soon as possible". As I followed the OC up the stairs the company Second-in-Command came to the top of the stairs near the ops room and said to the OC: "I've booked the helicopter for half past ten." I looked at my watch and it wasn't long to go and I thought that this must be a good job.

The OC ushered me into his office and told me to sit down. There was something not right in his demeanour or his face and he said those immortal words that I will never forget: "There's no easy way to say this, but your brother was killed by an IED in South Armagh this morning". I said "No". Everything just fell apart; there was a pause of disbelief. I dropped to a sofa armchair and just burst out crying uncontrollably. The OC was emotional too and he had to leave the office. He was gutted too and he knew it would be a body blow that I did not deserve. He'd told me in a professional manner and he didn't hesitate. His priority was to get me back to Rockwood and out of the Province quickly. I sat there still fully kitted up with my body armour, webbing and weapon and plenty of ammunition, just constantly crying to myself, in disbelief, not believing that Simon had been killed and I felt detached as I had lost a big part of my life, I no longer had the brother I looked up to, the only one I had.

I looked up to Simon in many ways but most importantly because he was older and more experienced than me and I respected him for being older. I respected him for having joined the army and giving me the influence, courage and support to do the same and follow in his footsteps. I had even attempted to join the Coldstream Guards but was rejected for my lack of height. Simon gave me the encouragement to continue in my attempt to join the army and I settled for a career I landed with and was happy with. Simon and I were not just brothers but good mates too and we had gone through a lot together, like the divorce of our parents and our separation that followed when I was 11 and Simon was 13. We supported each other and made sure we were OK. By the time we met up together in secondary school we had our own friends but would still look out for each other. When we met up on leave for a beer we would look after each other and reminisce. On the 17th August 1991 that opportunity, that routine and that friendship was taken away from me – a blow that I felt extremely hard to accept and hard to take in.

Over the years developments in Northern Ireland had turned many corners, but for me this journey came to a place that could never be turned back. If only those that dealt with it could imagine what they were doing to take away somebody so close, somebody who was a friend and a positive influence.

The CSM came in straight away and took my weapon and webbing off me. Perhaps he was thinking with safety in mind. After all, I had just been told that the IRA had murdered my brother and I had a weapon and 120 rounds of ammunition on me. He told me later "I took your rifle and ammunition off you to take the responsibility away from you, so that you could try and focus on what was now important. What was more important was to get you away from Northern Ireland as quickly as possible to support your family and this was not a place to grieve." Jamie's concerns and welfare issues were in the forefront of his mind, and rightly so in the role of the CSM, a role that he conducted so efficiently. He continued, "I was anxious you were able to travel quickly to your family, knowing they would be in need of your support." The OC came back into the room and I began to ask so many questions, questions that he did not know the answers to as it had only happened an hour or so before so he didn't know much. He had been told by the Adjutant that Simon had been killed instantly by a landmine and little remained of his body. With all good intentions and with a helicopter in-bound from Omagh the OC just wanted to get me out. He had tasked the CSM to fix my extraction out of Northern Ireland, which he did flawlessly. I remember the CSM telling me that I was earmarked for six weeks off, but of course if I needed more time then it was there. He had told me that the helicopter would fly me straight to London Heathrow where I would then be met and driven home. I didn't want to do that, as I needed to get back to Omagh to pack some kit, get out of my combats and to see Mel. He said that would be OK and that he would have to liaise with the pilot but my time would be short. Somebody took me from the Ops room to my accommodation, I couldn't remember who, as there was so much going on in my head. The powers that be had obviously decided I was not to be left alone – can't blame them really. I remember going into my room that I had shared with the rest of my section. My other three-team members that had come from Castlederg with me were all sat on the same bed on the left side of the room, dumbstruck and speechless with straight faces. They must have been thinking, "Shit, what do we say." My bags had been packed for me, but I had to laugh to myself as they had packed them so much that they had to tie my spare boots to the handle and had even placed my opened box of washing powder next to my kit, and I left the washing powder for them. I left the room and walked along the corridor, led by the CSM towards the heli-pad. The platoon commander, who was only a young 2nd Lieutenant and young in service, met me outside the room and he gave me a manly hug of condolence but couldn't say much else. I told him to make sure that the lads got back OK and to look after the platoon. The CSM led me to the heli-pad and soon after, I heard the distinctive hum of the helicopter in-bound. The sight of the helicopter became bigger and bigger until the Wessex was lowering to land on the heli-pad in the field adjacent to the SF base, surrounded by large oak trees which afforded a limited amount of cover from view next to the wide and fast-flowing River Derg. It was the most welcoming sound and sight at the end of every patrol, knowing it was coming to pick you up and take you back to your patrol base to get cleaned up and to enjoy some creature comforts until your next cold, wet and dark patrol. The CSM had a few words with me on the heli-pad as the chopper approached. It was not the same as a CSM to Corporal work related chat but it was a manly sympathetic one offering me support and comfort. The CSM was strict and thorough in his job and a lot of people were shy of him. It was clear where you stood as it was either black or white, and as long as you did your job and duties properly and professionally and didn't step out of line you were alright. He was the type of typically portrayed Sergeant Major that you wanted really. He told me how gutted he and the OC were and how every one else would be when word soon spread through the battalion. The Company and the command structure did all they could to help and the thoughts of the OC were that they couldn't linger for too long. Everyone felt for me on a personal loss but for operational reasons, had to move on.

I boarded the Wessex which flew me to Omagh. The door gunner handed me a pair of ear defenders for the journey. It felt strange for me to be in a helicopter on my own as I was so used to getting in one with the rest of my multiple. As it took off from the helipad at Rockwood, the door gunner, in the normal routine manner adopted the kneeling position and held the large machine gun and observed the area around as the helicopter reached a safe height. He then half-closed the door as it flew off towards Omagh. I recall just looking out of the door and flying over the beautiful countryside of Northern Ireland, the waters, the lush green fields, forests, hedgerows and mountains only bloodied again by the death of another soldier in the fight against terrorism. As I jumped out of the helicopter on the drill square at Omagh, I saw several friends and colleagues who had gathered waiting for the helicopter to land, each wanting to see or speak to me in their own way. I went straight to my room to quickly get changed and sort my self out. Tim, the company store man and accommodation NCO, stood at the entrance of the accommodation to let me in; as the company was away on Ops it had been locked. Tim, being the old and bold soldier stood in the foyer wearing his slippers, which was a common sight even in uniform. He must have got through so many over those years, but he had saved the army a load of money without issuing any boots. I was politely told that the helicopter had to go very soon. I got out of my uniform, throwing it on my room floor, got changed into my civvies and threw a load of stuff into a bag. I left my room in a right state but I didn't care. It was a short flight to Belfast airport, where I then boarded a domestic passenger flight to Heathrow. I don't recall being ushered anywhere at the airport. It was only an hour or so flight to London and I just sat there in my seat just wandering what and why whilst surrounded by people going about their normal business.

The plane landed at Heathrow, and then followed a cabin crew announcement, "Could passenger Ware please make himself known to the ground crew." Great!! I thought to myself. Who the hell am I supposed to speak to? Obviously someone on the ground, and fortunately there was a chap stood at the bottom of the aircraft steps, so I told him who I was and he led me into the terminal building and waited with me whilst the baggage was unloaded. He was obviously briefed as to what had gone on as he asked me how Simon had been killed and what happened. I told him the small facts that I knew, which at the time was not much. Once I had collected my bag I was led to a waiting unmarked military vehicle, which had been dispatched from Wellington Barracks to drive me home to Holt in Norfolk. It must have been the driver's most dreadful journey having to sit next to someone who he had never met before, for a two-hour journey whose brother had just been murdered. I remember every half hour the radio news reporting a Coldstream Guardsman being killed in South Armagh – another victim of The Troubles.

News of the incident had been reported very soon. At 9.50am the first TV crew arrived at the scene of the explosion, and by 10am the first news bulletin reported a bomb in South Armagh. The second bulletin at 11am reported that a Guardsman had been killed. Every time the news was broadcast the driver would turn the volume down but I told him it was alright to leave it as it was and listen to it, after all I had a lot more to cope with ahead.

He dropped me off at mum's house in Holt, and left soon after. I did consider the offer of a brew and something to eat but he agreed with me that the atmosphere was not going to be good and he chose the easy option to leave.

Simon's company commander, Christopher, was in the UK assisting in the training of the battalion who were to take over from the Coldstream Guards. He was at Stanford, a military training area in Norfolk and learnt of the tragedy from the CO by phone and was then sent to break the news to mum. He told me about that time he had the dreadful responsibility of breaking the news. He knew it needed careful handling for fear of saying the wrong thing and adding to the distress. Before he arrived at mum's house, he was aware that mum had heard the news as she had telephoned London District and was warned that somebody was en route. Christopher knocked on the door at around 12 o'clock, and he believed that as soon as the door opened, she knew before he could say anything. He then entered the house and passed the message onto my mother. Although shocked, he says that she was brave. He then stayed for about an hour and a half talking through Simon's job and the facts that he knew. Christopher was able to tell mum that Simon would have felt no pain and from information passed to him, the bomb would have killed him instantly. Christopher felt that this gave her some comfort, and having completed his task he left the house.

I don't recall the initial few hours but all the family were there and all were just asking questions to one and all and they would look to me for the answers and help. I couldn't answer them at this early stage as I only knew as much as them. I reassured them that being in the job that I was in then I would be able to find out. I was determined to.

We spent the rest of that day and night at home. The phone did not stop ringing, people were visiting and the television and radio was on constantly, awaiting every available news bulletin for updates. It was like I was gathering evidence. I remember the main late evening news at the time when the first pictures of the scene were transmitted on ITV. I saw the taped-off cordon sites and a large wooded area and I initially thought to myself, why had they been in the wood? But it was easy for me to criticise. I was not the patrol commander, I didn't know the area, and they could have been doing a routine patrol task in the wood for all I knew. The news reporter then reported a landmine explosion in excess of 250lb. I couldn't believe it, my early thoughts were maybe 50lb. Mum asked me what injuries Simon would have received. I had to be honest and say that if he were in close proximity of the device then his body probably would not be found. Her teacup and saucer smashed all over the floor. The family wanted answers and so did I, so I had to be honest from the start.

Simon's wife Carol wasn't told of his death until late that night. She had been on an army wives shopping trip to France and was told when the ferry arrived back in England at about 10pm. Carol was 24 at the time and only just married Simon in March of 1991 and had gone from a bride to a widow in just five months. The next day the news named Simon.

Keith R was the Families Officer who acted as the liaison between the regiment and the family, to help organise the funeral and sort out other welfare issues. He was a cheerful and very helpful man who kept us smiling as best he could, a man who maintained morale within the family, a man who made us laugh and a man who made us comfortable and relaxed. He was one of only a few men who I could count on one hand who gave us meaningful moral support throughout such a traumatic ordeal.

8

Simon is brought home

As I waited on the tarmac runway at London's Heathrow Airport Terminal One I saw the large doors of the luggage hold slowly open on what was a sunny afternoon. There in front of me, and only a few yards away I came the closest I was to Simon for many weeks as the coffin appeared from the hold of the aircraft ready to be received. The Coldstream Guards Families Officer, Keith, had done an enormous amount of organising to ensure that the funeral went smoothly and according to Carol's wishes. He was the liaison officer between the troops and the wives and in these circumstances was working hard and fast liaising closely with Carol and the family. He was a Captain who had worked his way up the ranks from a Guardsman with many years of hard work and therefore had the experience of soldiering and welfare life which assisted in his task and it was Keith's job to ensure everything went smoothly.

Simon would receive a full military funeral, which had to be planned along with Carol's and the family's wishes and Friday 23rd August was set as the day. I knew that before this, Simon had to be brought home to England. It's difficult to say 'brought home to British soil' as Northern Ireland is part of the United Kingdom even though he had been killed by Irish terrorists on British soil.

I remember watching the news footage from the Falklands war when the soldiers killed at Goose Green were buried in a mass grave shown on television. In 1982 it was before the time that soldiers' bodies were able to be flown or shipped home from the South Atlantic as it would take too long. After all, with exceptions to World War 1 and 2, there had not been many campaigns where soldiers' bodies were flown back to UK soil. That was the first time I observed on television what happens to Britain's war dead. It has only been since the Gulf War of 1991, the conflict in Bosnia, Afghanistan and the Gulf War that I have seen the live news coverage of those service men and women, having given their lives, being brought home with full military honours. The military precision of the scenes at RAF Brize Norton, RAF Lyneham and the parade through Wootton Bassett of the coffins draped in Union flags brings back all the emotions and memories of my own personal experience.

The first step was to meet Simon as his body, or rather what little remained of it, was returned from Northern Ireland. On the afternoon of Wednesday 21st August mum, Carol, Terry and I were taken in a minibus to Heathrow airport. Keith had ensured our timed and safe arrival at Heathrow and having met members of airport security staff we were escorted to a room in the terminal building to await the arrival of the plane. I don't recall how long we waited, but when the plane arrived we made our way to meet it. A second minibus contained the pallbearers, six in all including a senior NCO, all of whom were members of Simon's patrol that day.

A black hearse stood silent on the tarmac with its rear door open. Just then, a routine domestic British Airways flight from Belfast taxied to the terminal building. As it came to a halt the airport staff carrying out their daily tasks then attended to the plane. Mobile steps met each exit door, followed by a conveyor belt which met the doors of the baggage compartment. I watched as the door to the plane's hold opened slowly and before any of the baggage was offloaded, the coffin containing Simon emerged slowly into sight and was draped in a Union flag. The coffin was removed from the hold on the right side of the plane, along a conveyer belt and was picked up by the bearing party, consisting of six guardsmen in number 2 suits commanded by a senior NCO. Simon was then carried, at slow march only a few yards to the waiting hearse. I could see many onlookers stood watching in silent tribute and who would have realised that Simon was a soldier being received with military precision. Passengers leaving the plane, onlookers from the terminal building and airport staff all stood and watched. Not a regular occurrence. I had seen similar sights on television in similar situations and state funerals, but you never expect it to happen to you. The coffin was laid in the hearse with Simon's forage cap, belt and Northern Ireland medal which lay on top joined shortly after by a single red rose laid by Carol. I chose only to touch the coffin, the closest I would get to the regular handshake when Simon and I met up. The undertakers then closed the rear door of the hearse and once we were back in the minibus we then followed at slow speed off the runway out of the airport complex and then the road journey of a few miles to where Simon was then taken to rest at the Guards Chapel in Wellington Barracks central London.

There was no encouragement for Simon's body to be viewed at the Chapel of Rest simply because there was no body to view. Mum was advised against any viewing as the disruption of his body would be too distressing. Carol was told politely that viewing was not an option. I remember saying to Charlie that I knew Simon's body was not in the coffin as not much of it was found, and I felt that it was weighed down with sand to simulate body weight. One of the Pallbearers later admitted he thought it felt heavier than expected as they knew not much was found of Simon.

The night of 22nd August we had all stayed over at Simon and Carol's army flat in Balham. There were mum, Rhiannon, Lindsey, Carol and me. We sank a few beers and spoke about Simon and joked over many things until the early hours. The next morning Keith knocked on the door to inform us that the cars had arrived. Over the past week he had been a tower of strength and laughter to keep morale up, but now he was the serious and somber character helping us to be strong. The two funeral cars picked us all up on the morning of Friday 23rd August and made the journey to the Guards Chapel. We were driven through the main iron gates to the entrance steps outside. The last time I stood on those steps was only five months earlier on March 9th as Simon's best man on his and Carol's wedding day. I didn't expect an entourage of television and news reporters so I didn't hang around outside. I didn't expect or realise the phenomenal news media coverage and at the time I didn't want the attention. I was on an operational tour of Northern Ireland at the time and was concerned about any security issues, although the next day I was grateful for the news and media coverage in the national papers and the local and national television news. All the national tabloids and broadsheet papers reported the story very well. *The Sun* published a full-page report with a photo of Terry, mum, Carol and me coming out of the Chapel after and depicted me as a "family friend". Although I had a number two haircut and a regimental tie of the Royal Green Jackets it wasn't hard to spot me as a soldier. Many of my friends and colleagues told me when I returned to Northern Ireland, how annoyed they were when the *Sun* newspaper described me as a 'family friend'. I just shrugged it off knowing that the copies in question were being sold in Northern Ireland. Other papers such as the *Times* and *Independent* and other local papers reported positively.

Friday 23rd August at 10.30am the funeral service began. The chapel was packed, every seat taken up by Guardsmen in number two dress and tunics. I would guess at probably four hundred or so, there was not an empty seat. Dominating the front was Simon's coffin balanced on two wooden bipods still draped in the Union flag and appointments. I placed one of my regimental plaques on top of the coffin, touched the coffin for the last time and took my seat at the front. Father Michael Seed, the same person who had married Simon and Carol only five months earlier, conducted the funeral service, which would not have been an easy task. The service was introduced and welcomed by the Reverend John Barrie, Chaplain to the Household Division. Simon's company commander, Christopher, read the first lesson, *Thessalonians* 4 verses 13-18. There followed the first hymn *The Lord is my Shepherd*. Then the Gospel was read and reflections of Simon's short but eventful and enjoyable life read by the Reverend Kingsley Joyce, Chaplain of the 2nd Battalion Coldstream Guards. Further prayers and readings followed, and then everyone stood for the Last Post.

Thou shall not grow old as those that are left grow old. Age shall not weary them, nor the years condemn. At the going down of the sun and in the morning. We will remember them.

Simon's coffin is carried by the soldiers and comrades who were with him on that last patrol.

– a verse and sound that will always bring a lump to my throat. Every year I had attended the annual Remembrance Day parade at the cenotaph in Enfield, a compulsory parade too in the army, so it was all-too familiar to me.

There followed the sound of the lone bugler playing The Last Post and a two-minute silence, which was broken, by the sound of Reveille. The final hymn, *Thine be the Glory* was then sung, which Simon and I chose as a hymn for Dad's funeral only three years earlier, as it was one that he liked. Final prayers and commendation were said.

I recall a couple of years earlier that when I had visited Simon at Wellington barracks whilst he was on guard duty he showed me a coffin in one of the storerooms of the guard room. I learnt then that it was for rehearsals for funerals but Simon had never practiced with it, he never had the need, but no doubt it had been out a few times in the days leading up to Simon's funeral.

Following the service at the Guards Chapel, a funeral procession took Simon to the Lavender Hill Cemetery in Enfield – a journey of about ten miles through central London.

Leaving the Guards Chapel along with Carol, mum, my grandmother and step-dad Terry.

Passers-by, members of the public going about their daily business, watched the hearse drive by, draped in the Union Flag, probably not knowing who it was until watching the news later that day. Simon's plot was to be the same as our dad's, Dennis, who had died suddenly of a heart attack in March 1988. Simon's coffin arrived at the graveside and there followed a traditional short burial service with military honours – his body lowered slowly to rest. More people attended the burial, from Enfield, who could not make the service at the Chapel. They consisted of friends of Simon's and mine from school and representatives from the local Royal British Legion Enfield branch, who Dad was on the committee for and Simon used to visit. General Sir George Burns, Colonel Commandant of the Coldstream Guards went out of his way to speak to me, which was very nice. The next day I revisited to see a mass of floral tributes, flowers and wreaths laid on and around the graveside and spilling onto adjoining graves.

From the next day on it was time to get on with life and remembrance. Not a time to get over it but a time to get used to dealing with it and moving on and reflecting on the past and good times and knowing that a good part of my life was never to return. I had spent another week or so at home on leave, when I decided I wanted to head back to work. I had been away for six weeks and I wanted to get straight back into things.

Fellow Riflemen were coming up to me expressing their condolence and concern and offering a lot of true support. A number of people told me that they did not expect me back in Northern Ireland but I had wanted to get back and carry on as normal for Simon's sake and more importantly I wasn't going to let the terrorists get the better of me. I wasn't scared and I persevered with more determination to achieve my aim in Northern Ireland. I told this to a newspaper reporter of the *Eastern Daily Press* during an interview at home with mum, the week following Simon's death. Soon after my return to Northern Ireland I was summoned into the CSM office within a couple of days and he emphasised to me the concerns he had of my return and the effect on my family. He offered me an immediate transfer if I wanted one but I refused and think I earned some respect for remaining with the regiment.

Simon's graveside at Lavender Hill Cemetery, Enfield, North London the
day following his burial. He shares the same grave with our dad.

By the time I returned to operational duties I was determined to investigate what actually happened to Simon, but I knew that it was not going to be easy. I had told the CSM that I wanted to go to Bessbrook for a couple of days to find out more. Some colleagues expressed concern and some were even asking if I was 'for real' but my main objective was just to view the bomb scene and to get it into my head. I had learned a rumour that some days earlier a patrol had lost a collection of terrorist photographs, and that Simon's patrol was sent to find them. I was fuming to find, that if that was the truth, through someone's error Yankee One Zero Bravo had to go and find these photos, which resulted in the death of Simon. I also read the debrief notes from the OC No 4 (Ops) Company on the incident report, that Carrickovaddy Woods had previously been used by soldiers on a number of occasions. More specifically Yankee One Zero Bravo had used it only a few weeks before Simon was killed. It was also evident that litter had been left but I had to find out for myself all of these facts. My thoughts were that if you are to advertise to the terrorist that you use woods on a regular basis then they are going to plant explosive devices. Terrorists don't plant bombs in the middle of nowhere and hope for the best, they observe and note patterns that are set.

I managed to get to Bessbrook just before Christmas 1991 having had the transport arrangements made by my Company Sergeant Major. I respected him more for allowing me the time off from operations to go, as he didn't have to let me go at all but he knew it was personal for me. At 08:30hrs on Saturday 7 December 1991 I was driven to Bessbrook Mill from Omagh, a short journey of an hour or so. On arrival I was shown briefly around the Mill where Simon was based on his tour and spent a few hours in the Intelligence cell at battalion headquarters to do my own research into what had occurred. I was soon to experience my first taste of South Armagh as reports were coming in of a large explosion at Crossmaglen and a mortar base plate had been sited at Forkhill – another mortar attack.

At the time, the 1st Battalion the Royal Green Jackets were based at Bessbrook Mill so I was welcomed by fellow Riflemen. Fortunately for me a Rifleman who I joined with worked in the office, so I was made even more welcome again. I requested to view the reports and photos and was soon summoned to the Intelligence Officer who suggested that I should not, due to its graphic content. After all it was my choice to travel to South Armagh and investigate what happened and I told him in a polite way it was why I was there. He backed down and allowed me to continue.

I read and appraised myself but was shocked at the photos of the site. The first one showed a scale of the crater, with a soldier stood in it. It was five foot deep and a few metres wide. I couldn't believe the size of it. Several other photographs showed pieces of army equipment which were recovered. Another one that stuck in my mind was just the damaged barrel of the GPMG Simon was carrying and a few rounds of ammunition. A GPMG would probably weigh 30lbs with a belt of two hundred rounds of ammunition, a heavy and bulky weapon with only half the barrel found. As time went on I was more convinced that Simon's body would never be recovered. At midnight it was time to go to Newtownhamilton and I was instructed to get my kit and make my way to the heli-pad at Bessbrook Mill to be flown out. I had, as a matter of routine, been deployed with all my operational kit just in case something had happened.

I put on my webbing, my Bergen, then placed my helmet on my head and picked up my rifle. I then walked from the accommodation block, through the car park, passing the memorial garden on the left and through the front gates with the guardroom on the left. I crossed the road, under the protection of the cover-from-view screen, and entered the heli-pad to a waiting Wessex. I boarded the helicopter as it took off and flew me to Newtownhamilton. As it flew through the cold darkness it dawned on me that I had just walked the same route, with the same operational kit to go on a patrol in the Newtownhamilton area – it was exactly the same routine that Simon did on the afternoon of Thursday 15th August 1991.

I landed at the security force base at Newtownhamilton and was escorted to the Operations room to be greeted by the Company second-in-command, Captain Paul C. Paul was later to be my families' officer when I trained recruits two years later in 1993 in Newcastle. I was again made welcome by fellow Green Jackets and managed to get some sleep as it was going to be an early start the next morning.

The next morning was Sunday 8th December and at 07:30am we patrolled out from Newtownhamilton security force base across the countryside for a few miles. I was placed in the patrol as number three and followed the team as we patrolled south west of the town. Strangely enough, this was the same position in the team that Simon had taken on that fateful day. It was unfamiliar ground to me but the patrol and infantry skills that we needed to apply were just the same. I was covering someone's back as they covered mine. We approached Carrickovaddy Woods from the west in pretty much the same route that Simon's patrol had taken. We climbed over the high ground and as we contoured the crest there it was – a medium-size wooded feature next to the Carrickovaddy Road consisting of deep green trees, dense and well-defined. Except that almost in the centre of the woods there was something missing. A few trees that were destroyed in the explosion had created a hollow gap, enough to make out from where I observed that it was the spot where Simon was killed. I wasn't allowed to go in to the wood as it was locally out of use so soon after the explosion. The team I was with remained static for some time as they allowed me to make my own observations. The other two teams continued to patrol the area to maintain protection. Once I had finished what I wanted to see, we then returned to Newtownhamilton by about 1pm and were dropped back to Bessbrook to await my transport back to Omagh.

After the funeral, and when I heard the news that the device was 250lb I was sure the coffin did not carry much. I recalled reading the ATO report stating that he estimated the device to be 250lb and I managed to speak briefly to one of the ATO team at Bessbrook Mill who admitted to me that it was the worst explosion he had ever dealt with during his EOD career. I admired his honesty and in fact he had heard that I was in Bessbrook and went out of his way to find me and talk.

I left Bessbrook having satisfied myself that I now had a picture of the scene in my mind. I had also gleaned a little more information and facts of the circumstances of the explosion. However I knew then that I had more information and facts to find.

9

The investigation begins

After initial reaction and assessment following their attack Yankee One Zero Bravo began their immediate follow-up. For each and every member of the patrol this proved to be an immensely emotional and testing time for them under tense and tough conditions. Not only had they come under a violent terrorist attack but they had to deal with a member of the patrol and friend being killed. During this immediate follow-up, specific actions and standard operational procedures (SOP's) were conducted so that any immediate threat of further terrorist contact was eliminated, and once that was completed the subsequent follow-up began.

A clearance operation and major investigation began to ascertain firm facts and obtain forensic and witness evidence for the inquest and the murder investigation in an effort to bring those perpetrators to justice. The Commanding Officer heard the sound of the explosion from his office at Bessbrook Mill and it was not long before initial reports and details began to arrive in the Battalion Ops room.

The follow-up began with the immediate deployment of additional troops, equipment and other agencies consisting of the remainder of Number 4 Company from Bessbrook and Number 1 Company from Newtownhamilton. One of the first to arrive after the area had been initially cleared was the Regimental Medical Officer, a Captain who was a qualified practitioner serving in the Royal Army Medical Corps and who was attached to the Coldstream Guards for the tour of Northern Ireland.

> I had been informed that an explosion had occurred in the vicinity of a foot patrol and I arrived at Carrickovaddy Woods shortly after 8:30 am. Other members of the patrol had informed me that someone was missing and they had tried in vain to search. On my initial observations, I entered the wood from the Carrickovaddy Road side some distance from the scene of the explosion, and I soon identified fragments of chest webbing and other military equipment. The webbing was constructed of extremely strong and durable material and together with the comments made by the other patrol members of the severity of the explosion I gave reason to pronounce that Simon had in fact been killed in the explosion. Some hours later I conducted a further search and discovered several body parts but could not identify them as those of Simon.

Other agencies arrived and probably the most important of these agencies were the Ammunition Technician Officer (ATO) and his team, the Royal Engineer Search Team and the Royal Engineer Search Advisor who were responsible for the clearance and making the area safe to allow the search and forensic follow up to be conducted by the police. Soon after the ATO team was put on standby following a report from the Ops room of the explosion then the commanders began their planning of how to conduct their part of the operation.

The Commanding Officer flew from Battalion Headquarters at Bessbrook as soon as possible and as soon as sufficient detail was available. Having overflown the area he was dropped off on the ground at the incident control point to the western side of Carrickovaddy Wood. This had been set up by surviving members of the patrol and was now controlled by the Company Commander of Number 2 Company, Stephen, who commanded 2 Company's area of Newtownhamilton.

At 10:15hrs the Reconnaissance Intelligence Centre conducted an overflight of the contact area, more commonly known as the 'RIC' flight. This process is the overflight, by a fixed-wing Canberra aircraft, to photograph the area and make it easier for commanders on the ground to plan the clearance operation, enabling the planners to view the ground features from an aerial photograph. The flight was complete by 10:50hrs. At 10:25hrs the Incident Control Point was moved from the western side to the northern edge of the wood, which became the start point for ATO after their deployment and would give the agencies an easier more direct approach route along the track. This location would have been the point where Y10B would have exited Carrickovaddy Wood into the field and where the helicopter pick-up was planned. For the ICP location it would prove easier for agencies to approach the contact site. The method of initiation of the device was the main important concern at this stage as no command wire had been found, and the contact point was not in line of sight of any possible remote firing point, which eliminated any remote firing device. It too seemed unlikely that Simon, who had followed three other patrol members, would have triggered the explosion by stepping on a pressure pad or setting off a trip wire. At the time there was no obvious method of initiation.

The first specialist agencies began to arrive at 12:03hrs and by 13:13hrs all were present at the ICP. This then enabled ATO to begin his initial sweep of the area. This was a time-consuming and meticulous task that took about forty minutes and was then followed about twenty minutes later by isolation of an area up to 50 metres away to eliminate any possible command wires in place, which was conducted by the Royal Engineer Search Team (REST) and was again a time-consuming task.

The REST consisted of a team of six soldiers, all members of the Royal Engineers who were trained in high-risk searches of Northern Ireland. The team consisted of a team commander, who is a Corporal, and whose responsibility it was to be the command and control of the team. He monitored and commanded the search operation and was also responsible for the planning phase having liaised with the RESA. A team second-in-command, a Lance Corporal, was responsible to the team commander and was in charge of administering the team and whose task was to complete the Northern Ireland Search Record (NISR), one of the hardest jobs of any search team. The remaining four members were made up of Sappers (private soldiers are referred to as Sappers in the Royal Engineers). They were trained in the use of all the search equipment and responsible to the team commander and would conduct the search tasks. The clearance operation was, as normal, a slow and lengthy process and the ATO was not ready to receive remaining agencies until 15:35hrs, for an extended search.

From the ICP, once the sweep and isolation had taken place, ATO then began a route search towards the contact point. En route any choke points, such as culverts and fences, ditches and dykes were searched thoroughly, again a time-consuming task depending on the terrain and weather. In Carrickovaddy Wood tall thick trees with low branches, which made the search more difficult, slowed the search process down. It was for this reason that a chainsaw was lifted into the ICP to clear the trees and low branches. Once this search was completed the ATO and the RESA drew up their plan of how the search and clearance of the site would be conducted and at 16:08hrs the ATO conducted the first controlled explosion to eliminate any danger of a secondary device. The slow process continued into early evening and the situation report (SITREP) recorded on the incident log at 18:07hrs read:

A search was carried out at the seat of the explosion. It is believed that it will be quite late and the call signs may be out overnight. Re-supply will be needed.

At 20:27hrs the first Puma helicopters began to leave Bessbrook to begin the extraction of non-essential operational troops and equipment, with two Lynx helicopters remaining airborne as 'top cover' to protect the extraction. The first to be extracted were the specialist agencies such as ATO, REST, RESA, SOCO and WIS. By 21:00 the extraction was complete with all agencies returning to Bessbrook. The area was secured overnight by troops from Number One and Number Four Company in the form of static locations in trenches and satellite patrols protecting the static troops. A further SITREP on the incident log at 21:24hrs reported:

All call signs now settled for the night. It has now been confirmed that LCpl Ware has been murdered and all his family have been informed. All call signs have been informed that a further day will be needed so the whole area can be sifted through for forensic evidence.

Day two of the clearance operation began and at 06:28hrs on Sunday 18th August the insertion of all agencies was complete on the ground and by 06:45hrs the clearance operation continued. The RUC search teams began a shoulder-to-shoulder and fingertip search of the area and the crater. One of the search teams was conducting a search of a garden very close to the edge of the woodland for further evidence. Later in the morning when the area was cleared, shouting was heard indicating that something had been found – it was Simon's sleeping bag from his Bergen found in a tree. Day two's operation was not as long and detailed as the first, and by 13:36hrs all agencies and call signs had been extracted back to their relevant locations.

A Higher Scientific Forensic Officer of the Northern Ireland Forensic Science Laboratory attended the scene at the request of the RUC. As far as terrorist crime is concerned, the RUC have the world's best forensic science department.

I was aware that there had been a fatal explosion, and described the site as next to a pathway in a wooded area close to the Carrickovaddy Road. On assessment I observed a large crater 5.6 metres in diameter and 1.6 metres deep at the side of the pathway in a grass bank to the right. Debris had been spread over a wide area and several trees around the crater had been damaged and some uprooted. I also observed a 10 metre length of twin flex cable and several pieces of flesh and bone close to the scene. Several items were recovered from the scene for forensic examination. These items included samples of soil, fragments of plastic and non-ferrous metals consistent with being a battery pack, fragments of plastic bin bags and fertilizer bags. Other items of wire, wood and ferrous metal were also recovered.

He went onto summarise:

From my examination of the scene and of the items recovered, I am of the opinion that a charge of explosive in the order of 200-300lbs, possibly contained in a galvanised container, functioned in the bank. The deceased would have been in close proximity to the device when it functioned. Although the exact construction of the device could not be fully determined it incorporated two headlamp batteries giving a 12 volt supply and a loop of wire possibly as a 'safe to arm' connection. A similar wire arrangement has been encountered in two recent devices, where it was part of an improvised electronic circuit, which functions as a victim-operated booby trap. The damage and condition of the battery fragments is consistent with a charge of high explosive having functioned close to them and would tend to indicate a self-destruct mechanism may also have been present as part of the device.

On the same day a civilian Scenes of Crime Officer (SOCO) who at the time was based at Newry RUC station attended the scene. He had been directed to attend by the RUC Detective Sergeant, who had informed him that Cpl Ware had been killed in an explosion. On arrival and once the Army ATO declared the area safe the SOCO assisted the Higher Scientific Forensic Officer in the search of the area.

I was directed to search the woods for the remains of Simon Ware, along with the assistance of the RMO who earlier attended and the RUC search teams. During the search of the area I found the following remains: – both feet still in their boots 84 feet from the crater, both femurs (thigh bones) both of which were found in a tree, one

Part of the twin flex cable used in the detonation of the device is recovered from the scene.

located about 40 feet and the other 110 feet from the crater, a knee joint, skin from the abdomen, left mandible, a small fragment of skull and various pieces of muscle and threaded clothing and equipment, which had been scattered over a wide area within the wood. The furthest piece of flesh I located was over 300 feet from the site of the explosion. At 8:30pm I left the scene and an hour later attended the mortuary at Daisey Hill hospital where the remains were deposited. The next day, the 18th August, I re-attended the scene and continued the examination of the site. Whilst examining an area to the rear of the crater I was called to the far side of the wood, on the western side, some 330 feet away to a field where a search team had found Simon's left hand with the arm intact. Simon's wedding ring was still on his finger.

It was of great sentimental value that his wedding ring was found and returned to Carol. Simon also wore another ring, which was never found. It was our dad's signet ring, which had his initials, DRW engraved on it. Because Simon's right hand was not recovered, it was presumed that this was the reason why. In fact the ring was too big for Simon's fingers, so that he carried the ring on his identification tags around his neck, which were never found either. The SOCO later re-attended the mortuary with further remains, which were handed to the pathologist for the post mortem.

The military equipment recovered from the scene was later returned to the Coldstream Guards at Bessbrook for their disposal.

The scene was attended and examined by other agencies that reported pretty much the same. A medical practitioner attended Daisey Hill mortuary at the request of the police and was handed two plastic bags, which contained the remains of Simon that had been found at the scene over the past two days. They were officially identified as Simon through dental records and fingerprints and life was pronounced extinct at 9:50pm on Sunday 18th August 1991.

In all a total of in excess of 100 ground troops and five helicopters were involved in the security, clearance and deployment of troops over the two-day clearance and search operation. In addition to the ATO, other specialist agencies were deployed to assist in the clearance, which consisted of a Royal Engineers Search Team, a Royal Engineers Search Advisor, Weapons Intelligence Section, Scenes of Crime Officers and Forensic Scientific Examiners and the RUC's Divisional Mobile Support Unit. The police in the Irish Republic, the Garda, were informed of the incident soon after, but took no involvement.

There was a lot to be learnt from this serious incident. In the initial debrief and as a result of evidence and information gleaned from the clearance operation and the weeks following it would become clear that certain procedures, personal skills and patrol techniques might have to differ. There were certain comments and considerations and there was much concern about the IRA's ability to construct and initiate such devices.

The Weapons Intelligence Section reported that the explosion in Carrickovaddy woods bore many similarities to the explosion in Crossmaglen on 4th June 1991 that injured a L/Sgt from Number One Company. This explosion occurred in a field adjacent to the Newtown Road, Crossmaglen as the patrol crossed a field. Again there was no initiation established however a length of cable was recovered. On the 18th June 1991 a soldier was injured when an explosion occurred on the Finiskin Road, Cullyhanna. Again no form of initiation was identified however a length of cable had been recovered. On the 4th July 1991 an explosion site was discovered by an army patrol in the area of Recklan

Road, Cappagh, Co Tyrone. Many items of forensic interest were recovered, in particular a length of electrical cable, biscuit tin and the remains of a Mark 15 Timer Power Unit (TPU). On the 12th September 1991 in a field off the Drumlough Road, Crossmaglen, an IED comprising of 212kg of HME was recovered. Again no form of initiation was discovered, however a length of twin flex cable was recovered.

These all bore the similarities to the construction of the device that killed Simon. All of them had no form of initiation discovered which concludes that they all could have been/were victim-operated and all in the same area. Initial comments in relation to the murder of Simon state that the device was designed to kill and was built deep into the bank to cause maximum effect and was likely to be victim-operated.

There were five main lessons that could be learnt from this attack:

1. The spacing of the patrol was sufficient to deny the enemy more than one serious casualty or fatality.
2. Areas which are attractive to soldiers, frequently visited and showing signs of previous patrol presence, must be avoided.
3. The area surrounding isolated derelicts should be avoided. (Although the 1:25000 scale map of Carrickovaddy Wood shows a derelict within 10m of the contact point, it was in fact not present on the ground on 17 August 1991)
4. Patrol route selection must avoid being channeled through areas of very limited access.
5. Litter and signs of presence of troops in an area must be eradicated.

It was plainly most unfortunate that the patrol used the track through the wood that day and careful avoidance of similar areas should minimise the risk of a reoccurrence.

10

Recovery

The recovery from Simon's death, or should I say, the dealing with it, would be a massive hurdle for all of us to handle in our own individual way. It was really not a time to recover, but a time to get used to coping with the loss of a son, brother, nephew, husband and friend. We weren't going to get over it, but had to get used to it. Simon's death was the latest in a recent spate of terrorist-related deaths in Northern Ireland that brought the total number to eight in eight days with Simon being the first, and five of those were in the first 48 hour period. This was a time when the Government was considering reintroducing Internment, a difficult tactical action which would not solve the violence but could have been a short-term solution to an ever-increasing problem of terrorist violence. A senior police officer described the time as "A serious situation but not a catastrophic one". He suggested that the army and the RUC would "Robustly handle the situation". It seemed there was a death every day in the fresh wave of violence, which was one of the worst outbreaks for several years.

Seven other families were experiencing the same sadness, trauma and heartache that we were, with the loss of a relative and friend. Not all of the deaths were soldiers and none of them deserved it. Simon became another name on the list for the roll of honour and a statistic on the death toll, leaving another murder to be investigated by the police.

Simon's death would not have been expected to have had any reflection on how things may or may not have changed the situation in Northern Ireland nor was it expected to have any media emphasis. However I was surprised that the next day Simon and our family would feature in virtually all the national newspapers, all of which reported well and sensitively. The weekly local papers too led well with the same story ..."Another victim of the troubles". Most of the nationals emphasised that Simon was a Catholic victim of an IRA booby trap. This would have no effect on the terrorists as they felt the army was a threat to them and were intruders on their soil, and that there was no concern over what religion they were. The photograph the MOD released via the press office showed Simon on his wedding day in his ceremonial red tunic and holding his bearskin in his right arm – the uniform world-famously known and proudly worn by those soldiers of the Guards Division, whose main attraction draws thousands of tourists to London, the pictures that appear on souvenir postcards of London and the photo taken on his wedding day outside the Guards Chapel.

Over the following days we received many letters of condolence and support from people of all walks of life, expressing themselves over our loss. People who had never met us and those that didn't know what we were experiencing and those that did not know any different. The first one I received was from my Commanding Officer and was given to me before I left Omagh to fly home that day. Mum received many more, one in particular from Sir Alastair Aird, Controller of the Household at Clarence House, the home of the Queen Mother, expressing how much the Queen Mother was upset over the news. Simon had once completed an attachment to Clarence House for several weeks and was very fond of the Queen Mother. Many of the letters helped in mum's recovery with all the support and kindness given, many of them from strangers who had lost family members in tragic circumstances. More were from local people expressing support mum described as "absolutely tremendous".

As the days went by I became more aware that Simon's death was nationwide headlines on the news as well. He was an ordinary soldier, like the many others, but the media wanted to emphasise the tragedy. We were keen for this to happen as we did not want Simon to be forgotten and we wanted the nation to realise that all the violence and loss is unnecessary.

Mum had received several phone calls from various newspapers all interested in reporting the story. She chose to have a short interview at home a couple of days after his death with a reporter from the *Eastern Daily Press*, a local Norfolk paper. The media attention on the day of the funeral was a surprise too, and it wasn't until that day that I became aware of it.

When we got out of the funeral cars outside the Guards Chapel, shortly before 10:30am on that Friday morning, we were greeted by a line of photographers and camera crews. Even though I was not expecting it I was surprised but pleased that they were there as I was keen for the incident to be publicised. The reporters were respectful as none of them approached us for any comment. This day meant that the following day's newspapers would carry the news of Simon's funeral and the lunchtime and evening national news led with the story and footage of the family leaving the cars and entering the Guards Chapel. The following morning I recall going into WH Smith's in the Enfield town shopping precinct to see what the headlines were and to my utter surprise and amazement the *Sun* depicted a full-page coloured article titled.."From bride to widow in 5 months". The story had three photos – one of mum, Carol, me, Terry, Uncle Phil and my grandmother leaving the chapel; underneath that, one of Simon's coffin being carried; followed by one of the coffin being placed in the hearse. *The Times* led with the heading ..."Buried soldier victim of evil". All the papers carried similar stories, so I bought the lot and the shop assistant must have thought I was bored. Later that day I read all the articles and have kept them to this day. All the stories spoke well of Simon and, not to forget, they connected others that have been lost too under similar circumstances. The following day I visited my local pub, *The Enfield Arms*, next to Enfield Town train station, a pub which had been my local for three or four years with many a weekend visit or three. The pub was run by the parents of two girls that I went to the same primary school with and I remember talking to their mother one evening and had taken in some photos of Simon and Carol's wedding, as she had asked to see them. As she looked at them, a couple of unknown customers nearby had recognised the photo in the newspaper and briefly spoke to me. It was nice to see that people had recognised Simon.

The days and weeks following were spent trying to come to terms with what had happened and to get on with life, which would not have been easy but we had to move on and deal with the future. It would be something that we would never get over but after the busy last two weeks of dealing with the death and the funeral, it now seemed there was a lull, a time to move on. I was asked several times over my plan and intention to return to Northern Ireland or even to stay in the army. I made it clear from the beginning that I would not leave the army as a result of this and I would not transfer from my regiment and certainly would be returning to Northern Ireland to complete my operational tour with added determination. It was what I wanted to do and it was what Simon would have wished for. I was not going to let the terrorists get the better of me and, I was not going to concede and secondly I had a lot of friends in the battalion that would be supportive. I did not want to shy away from the threat of Northern Ireland or the threat of the terrorists, the best thing to do I thought, was to carry on, confront the threat and get on with it. It was my way of recovering and trying to deal with it.

The day I returned to Omagh on the 14th September was discrete, as I did not want a big welcome back. I had told the Company Sergeant Major that I wanted to return early and to get on with life. I arrived by mid-afternoon and had decided to go to the NAAFI and the Corporals' Mess that night for a few beers just to break the ice and settle back in. As I walked into a half-full bar area the quietness hit me as we walked towards the bar. I vividly remember 'Sibo', a corporal from Support Company who I had worked with a lot before, leave his seat to greet me before I reached the bar, with a handshake and comments of condolence. 'Sibo' was a confident, strong person with good character which I respected him for. That I think broke the ice, as he bought me a pint and then I spent the night talking to a lot of people about what had happened. People didn't know the whole story and they wanted to know and I wanted to tell them.

As the months and years went by we all had a different way of dealing and coping with it. My intention was to get on with army life, work and lifestyle and openly talk about Simon's incident. When mum died in February 1994 I came across a small writing book whilst clearing out her belongings, a type of schoolbook used for story writing at primary school. There was a title on the front, which said 'Book of Dreams'. Intrigued to its content I opened it to find three paragraphs. The first described a time in our house at Clarence Road, Ponders End in Enfield where mum had seen Simon at the top of the stairs. Mum had walked from the living room to the open-plan dining room where, by the front door, was an open staircase to the right. Simon appeared sitting at the top of the stairs but as mum approached he disappeared. The other brief paragraph described a situation whereby mum visualised a large orange flash, similar to that of an explosion, and then she woke in bed. The third entry was in more detail. Mum and Carol visited Simon's grave together one afternoon with some plants for the grave and they had taken a small gardening trowel to dig them in. As mum began to dig a few inches below the surface she revealed the lid of the coffin. They continued to dig the earth and remove the coffin lid. Mum then describes seeing Simon 'asleep' in the coffin saying "Don't disturb me" as he turned over. It was the psychological and emotional effect that it had on mum's mind. As if his murder and funeral was not hard enough there was the heartache of horrible dreams and nightmares that just kept reminding her.

There may have been more but they were not written down and it must be hard for any mother to feel the loss of a child. Mum had said to me on more than one occasion that it was hard for her – after all, she carried Simon for nine months and then gave birth, so it was as if a part of her was dead.

There have been many who were involved on that day who never replied to my letters and it may have been that over the years they had moved on. On the other hand they may not have wanted to remind themselves of that horrible day and who could blame them? Many of them no doubt have reoccurring memories either good or bad that still trouble them to this day. One told me that there was an enormous amount of gut-feeling – hatred, vengeance, anger, 'what are we doing here?' Waste, sitting ducks, 'round up all the terrorists and shoot them' – from a soldier in sight of the explosion. Another went onto say "I still think of what happened that day, not too often, but now and again and it's always that hole in the ground and those colours I don't think I will ever forget".

Many will take the images and experiences to their graves, some wishing they had told their story and some wishing not to repeat the trauma of what they had seen on that day, and the images that haunted them afterwards.

11

The Inquest

It was now March 1993 and I had just begun a two and a half year posting to the Infantry Training Battalion at Ouston near Newcastle-upon-Tyne, where I was training recruits from both the Royal Green Jackets and the Light Infantry. The previous year I had been sent on the Section Commanders' Battle Course (SCBC), which I thought was surprisingly earlier than expected, as I didn't expect to go on the course for another year or so. The course was run by the Small Arms School Corps (SASC) and the Infantry Training Wing at Brecon in Wales. All infantry soldiers are required to complete the SCBC in order to get promoted to Corporal and become a section commander. The course consisted of six weeks at Strensall near York on Phase 1, which included weapon instruction and range conduct and safety whilst running a shooting range and supervising live firing exercises. The second six weeks on Phase 2 consisted of infantry tactics instruction in Brecon. On successful completion at the end of the course, not only were you glad to get away from rain-drenched and hilly Wales, but successful students were then qualified to get promoted to the rank of Corporal and would conduct weapon and tactics instruction and command a section of eight men, and if required in the absence of a platoon sergeant, then command the platoon of up to thirty four men in the infantry role.

The training depot was a big step for me. I had been promoted to corporal and was training recruits how to become soldiers and I was only 21. Young, yes, but I had already done two tours of Northern Ireland and plenty of complex exercises in the UK and overseas with added trust and responsibility.

On one exercise in Canada in 1990 I had been selected to become the Commanding Officer in the final exercise and lead the whole battalion, about 600 men on a deliberate attack and I was only 19. I was even given the use of a helicopter and its pilot for doing some recces. My superiors obviously thought I had the knowledge and confidence, and over the past 18 months to 2 years as a strong Rifleman I had proved that I had good qualities of leadership, command and control and enthusiasm. So much so, that they had given me the responsibility of commanding the battalion of 600 men for four hours.

I felt I was quickly sent on the section commander's battle course to get me out of Northern Ireland for three months, but on my return I did not get the impression that I jumped the queue for promotion. I was not complaining, after all, it would give me promotion and more money, but it meant twelve weeks away.

I always kept a framed photo of Simon and me in my room, which was taken on his wedding day outside Wellington Barracks. Simon was stood on the left and looked very proud, dressed in his red tunic and holding his bearskin in his right arm and there was I in my Number two dress. I took it everywhere. On one occasion during the Phase 1 of SCBC the instructors conducted one of many routine room inspections. All instructors on the SCBC were senior NCO's recruited from many infantry regiments but all wore the SASC cap badge and beret. One of the sergeants inspected the four-man room that I was in and his attention was drawn to the photograph above my bed. Not recognising the likeness of Simon and me he looked twice at the photograph, pointed to the soldier in the red ceremonial tunic and asked if I knew him. I told him that he was my brother. His face dropped with an obvious lump in his throat. He removed his glove from his right hand and offered it out to me in a handshake of condolence. He told me that he had known Simon and served with him in the 1st Battalion Coldstream Guards. It's a small world and it gave some hope that Simon was recognised and not forgotten.

I received a letter via the military post one day inviting me to attend the inquest into Simon's death. It informed me that Carol had waived her right to attend the inquest and asked if I wanted to attend instead. Carol had declined the offer to attend so soon after Simon's death, as she did not feel up to going, which was understandable. At the time I was unaware of what the procedure of an inquest was, but I soon found out and expressed my wish to attend. I'd never been to an inquest before and didn't know what to expect. It was held at Bamber Court House in County Down, Northern Ireland and after a short flight to Belfast I was met by a military escort and accommodated at Aldergrove military airport and driven to the court the next day.

On arrival at the Court we waited in the public waiting area prior to the inquest in a small room with some vending machines and quite a few other members of the public, whose attention was drawn to me. Whether it was because I may have stood out as a soldier being in the company of other police officers I don't know, but I was concerned

Simon and me on his wedding day two days before he deployed to South Armagh. On the steps of the Guards Chapel, Wellington Barracks, London.

as we were waiting with other members of the public. I was in a public place in Northern Ireland, still in the army and not armed and out of my comfort zone, which caused me some concern, but nevertheless we were first in the courtroom.

Just prior to the beginning of the inquest I was spoken to by the Detective Sergeant from the RUC Criminal Investigation Department who had been involved in the murder investigation and examination of the bomb scene. He told me that the details of some statements and reports were graphic and I may find them to be disturbing when read out during the inquest but, having spoken to members of the patrol at Simon's funeral, I was of the conclusion that there would not have been much left of his body, and I was aware of the ferocity of the explosion.

It was the first time I had been in a courtroom and learned it was not a judge that presided over the inquest, but a Coroner. As I entered the courtroom I was met by an environment that I had not seen before. Long dark wooden benches laid out in different formations and different directions all focused on the centre of the court and the main chair situated at the centre front of the courtroom. This chair was occupied and dominated by the Coroner. Other benches were occupied by family, expert witnesses, media and members of the public, everyone wanting to know what was being discussed. I remember the coroner calling the individual witnesses, the police, the scenes of crime officers and the pathologist, each giving their evidence and version of events in graphic detail. The Coroner summed up on behalf of all those involved in the investigation, and gave sympathy and regret over what had happened, and it gave me some little comfort. The inquest was over after a short time and a verdict of "open verdict" was concluded.

I was disappointed at the decision and was informed that the coroner's inquest was only to ascertain the cause of death and not to apportion blame on any individual. That would be the job of the criminal court. The cause of death was clear and informed by the coroner and endorsed on the death certificate as:

1(a) Multiple injuries due to
 (b) Bomb explosion

The pathologist then summarised his report as follows:

Shortly after 07:30hrs on the 17th August 1991, the deceased was walking along a track in Carrickovaddy Wood, South Armagh. He was the third man of a four-man patrol walking in single file when an IED, concealed in a bank on his right and in close proximity to him, detonated, killing him instantly and completely disrupting his body. It was believed that the device was planted by the Provisional Irish Republican Army, a prescribed organisation, and death would have been instantaneous. In the evening of 17th August 1991 the remains were escorted to the mortuary at Daisy Hill hospital by the Detective Sergeant from the RUC CID and identified as the remains of Simon. External examination showed that the body was completely disrupted, with large portions that had disappeared.

With the lack of forensic evidence from the scene and no arrests, the blame could not be directed at any individual, but bore all the hallmarks of an IRA attack. How reliable it is to this day I don't know, but some months later I was approached in Strabane police station by a member of military intelligence to tell me that the terrorist believed responsible for the planting the bomb that killed Simon was shot dead in an Army operation in

Coalisland on 16th February 1992. I was given the details of him, a young IRA terrorist, but I decline to mention his name without confirmation. You can imagine how I felt.

I wrote to the Coroner on my return and requested all the statements and reports that were used to ascertain the cause of death. The reports and statements arrived soon after my request and were gruesome and graphic, but to the point. They were not written in a sensitive way to upset me, they were written for evidential purposes.

12

A lasting memory

By the beginning of 1993 Simon had been gone for 18 months, and at that time I recall talking to my mother about having lost Simon and that a lasting memory was deserved. Knowing that there are many local and national war memorials depicting names of soldiers of the two World Wars, I also knew that not many of those local service men and women who had given their lives in other worldwide recent conflicts were visibly remembered. I felt that these soldiers should be recognised for what they had given. We were disappointed about Simon's name not being included on the war memorial in Enfield and felt that he deserved some recognisable respect.

Mum was slowly deteriorating with breast cancer and having more visits to the hospital for her treatment. It placed a great strain on her health and welfare, more than I was aware of really, as I knew that she would not want to worry about both of us and that's why she kept it quiet.

I took it upon myself to write to the government and at 22 years old, a corporal in the army but not well up with politics, I wanted to make my point and views heard. Well, I didn't know much about politics, as I wasn't really interested in it but I should have been really as it was politics and the government that sent me to Northern Ireland to fight terrorism in the first place! My letter was directed to my local MP for Enfield and in it I explained what had happened to Simon and that I felt his name along with others should be on the local Cenotaph. After all, for many years my mum and dad had taken us to the annual Remembrance Day parade to pay respects to the war dead, as many people do. Surprisingly I got a speedy reply. It was only a couple of weeks later that a headed envelope from Parliament dropped in my letterbox of the house I lived at in Newcastle. It wasn't from the Member of Parliament personally, but from a personal aide and it read that the matter had been passed on for approval. I believe that to this day that he probably didn't read the letter that I wrote and that it was either put on the bottom of the pile of paperwork or briefly mentioned in conversation. Months, and in fact years passed, I never did get a reply and I lived in that same house for two more years – no similar envelope landed on my door, so in the end I gave up.

By December of 1993 mum had got progressively worse with cancer and for a week or two she had a bed next to my grandmother, who too was suffering from throat cancer, at the Norfolk and Norwich Hospital the week before Christmas. Christmas passed and although mum put on a brave face when we spoke and a brave face when we visited, she couldn't do it forever and her health deteriorated. I remember the phone call that morning. I was in the office at work having a briefing before taking the recruits out on an adventure training day and looking forward to a long mountain bike ride. The phone rang and I was called to the CSM's office. I was told that mum had gone into a coma in hospital, which didn't sound promising, and I was sent home from work. I went home and quickly packed and made that long worrying journey to Norfolk from Newcastle, which took about five hours. Fortunately we didn't have any children to worry about, and we traveled straight to hospital before teatime. Mum had been moved to a side room and I knew the worst was on its way. It was a small room with all the family spending most of the time with her there. There was not much the staff could do really; she had been pumped up with morphine so at least it wasn't painful, for her anyway. As this was my first visit to mum, Terry had asked if one of the nurses could update me as to mum's condition. Terry accompanied me to a side room with the nurse, Terry still holding his cup and saucer of tea and in a nutshell the nurse said that there was not much that they could do for mum really. Terry's cup started to wobble as he got upset and unbalanced. I had flashbacks of the time mum's cup and saucer smashed at home when I told her that Simon's body would not be found, so I took it off him and placed it on the table.

By early evening we had decided to go out to get some food, as we hadn't eaten for a while. I told mum what our plans were and she reacted in a way that was strange, by lifting her head and shoulders off the pillow and raising her right arm and pointing to the ceiling. She mumbled an unrecognizable sentence and I said that we would not be long. We got some fish and chips and went to mum's house to eat them but by the time we got there, there was an answerphone message from Carol, who had been called by Terry, telling us to get back to the hospital quickly. We drove back as quickly as we could and went straight back to the room we had left earlier, in the same condition. Mum was clearly in her last moments of her life and there, shortly after 8pm on 3rd February 1994, I watched her take her last breath as she died. This was hard for me as I had lost my brother and watched my mother die in the space of two and a half years.

I never got round to chasing up the politicians as I didn't have too much hope and I had other things to worry about. Six weeks later my grandmother died of cancer, followed in the spring of 1995 by my stepfather Terry, who died of leukemia. I never got back on track with it from there. After all, losing four close family members in four years was a bit of a blow and people wondered how I would cope.

By the end of the summer of 1996 I was almost half-way through an operational tour of Bosnia when I received a letter from the Quartermaster of the 1st Battalion Coldstream Guards. He informed me that whilst the battalion was on a further tour of South Armagh they had erected a stone memorial to Simon in the garden of remembrance at Bessbrook Mill on the 17th September 1996. A service had been conducted and the memorial was dedicated by the services' Catholic chaplain based at Portadown – photos of the memorial service were enclosed.

On the tenth anniversary in August 2001 the Regimental Sergeant Major, Commanding Officer and other members of the Battalion who were on the patrol that fateful day in 1991 flew back to Bessbrook to hold a small service and to lay a wreath at the memorial stone, which I thought was fantastic.

From 2001 a number of military security force bases became scaled down and in April 2007 the Army's last patrol returned to Bessbrook Mill and the Mill was officially handed back to the local authority after years of military use. On 31 July 2007 Operation Banner, the British Army's operation in Northern Ireland, came to an end after 38 years. Thousands of soldiers had deployed from 'The Mill' and thousands of helicopters had conducted many sorties too. I received a phone call soon after from the Brigade Commander's second-in-command informing me that Simon's memorial stone was removed from the grounds, and that a rededication service would be conducted to relocate it at Thiepval Barracks, the Headquarters of Northern Ireland.

The memorial stone at Bessbrook Mill.

I had earlier read with interest a letter to the editor of the *Sunday Express* on 31 December 2000 from Rita Restorick suggesting the government should honour the servicemen and women of Northern Ireland with posthumous medals in recognition of their lives. Her son, Stephen Restorick, a Lance Bombardier in the 3rd Regiment The Royal Horse Artillery, was the last soldier to be killed in Northern Ireland by the Provisional IRA. Stephen was talking to a motorist at the vehicle check point at Bessbrook Mill, Lorraine McElroy, a local Catholic women living in Bessbrook who he had stopped at the checkpoint on the evening of the 12th February 1997. He was shot by a terrorist sniper who fired a Barrett .50 calibre sniper rifle from the boot of a car about 200 yards up the road from the checkpoint. Lorraine was slightly injured in the attack but Stephen was fatally wounded and died a short time later at Daisy Hill Hospital. I replied to the letter with support regarding her campaign.

Rita told me at the beginning of 2002 about the Ulster Ash Grove, in The National Memorial Arboretum, which is a large memorial park off the A34 near to Alrewas in Staffordshire, located in a disused gravel works with different sections for each war and campaign and for each different regiment.

It is a large area of peaceful countryside and the Ulster Ash Grove is a fairly new addition in recent years, created in 2001 – in memory of each soldier killed in Northern Ireland there is an ash tree planted. Rita and John had visited Stephen's tree and had told me where Simon's was. I was grateful to be told and very happy to know that Simon had been recognised once again in another national memorial and a little closer to home. We traveled down a few days later. The weather was appalling that day and we didn't predict the wind and rain and weren't even dressed for it either. We found the location of the Ash Grove and we traipsed through the long wet grass to locate Simon's tree, which we found after a short time. There it stood, about eight feet tall, young, and with a small plastic plaque attached to it which read:

The Ash tree at the Ulster Ash Grove at the National Memorial Arboretum, Staffordshire.

Planted for LCpl Simon Ware
Coldstream Guards
17th August 1991 22yrs

I felt good to be a little closer to his memory and to see his name recognised. At the end of 2001 and the beginning of 2002 the memorial attempt took a step closer as my stepsister, Kate, had told me that she had instigated an attempt to have Simon's name engraved on the Holt town war memorial in Norfolk. In 1997 the government announced that local councils were able to have the names of local soldiers who had died in other campaigns other than both World Wars, to be inscribed on local war memorials. After all, my mum had moved to the town in 1988. I didn't hold out too much hope, as I hadn't had much success in the past but Kate convinced me that it would happen. She had contacted several councillors to organise it and in turn they had contacted me. It seemed to have been sorted fairly quickly and a memorial date was set for later in the year. Ron Stone, the project coordinator along with Joan, who lived only a few doors up from mum and Terry, had put a lot of effort in with meetings and organisation. The the engraving of Simon's name on the war memorial cost the council £400 and a fresh stone memorial was erected in St Andrew's church, Holt. I was happy to put a large contribution towards the cost.

September 1st 2002 was the date set for the dedication of the church memorial. Ron Stone had spoken to me on the phone and told me that it would be part of the Sunday morning service. I didn't expect it to be a big affair, but I was to be proved wrong. Ron met us in the church foyer just before the service, where he showed us the book of remembrance with Simon's epitaph in it. Sat at the front of the church were two of Simon's colleagues in ceremonial tunics and a regimental bugler dressed the same, who had traveled from Chelsea Barracks to be there, which would have been an early start for them. It was an extremely moving service, conducted by Father Howard Stoker. I was fine until the dedication of the memorial stone and the last post. It brought back memories of the 23rd August 1991 – the day of Simon's funeral. The bugler sounded the last post, followed by the 2 minutes silence and then reveille. This was a sequence of events I had experienced many times before. I read a short poem for Simon before the service concluded.

Do not stand at my grave and weep,
I am not there, I do not sleep.
I am a thousand winds that blow,
I am the diamond glints of snow,
I am the sunlight on ripened grain,
I am the gentle autumn rain,

When you wake in the morning's hush,
I am the swift uplifting rush,
Of quiet birds in circled flight,
I am the soft stars that shine in the night,
Do not stand at my grave and cry,
I am not there, I did not die.

The plaque erected soon after Simon's death inside the Guards Chapel on the West Wall.

This poem, written by Mary Elizabeth Frye, reminds me also of Lance Bombardier Stephen Cummins, who was killed near to Londonderry, Northern Ireland, in 1989. He had written it down and given it to his parents shortly before his death, in the form of a sealed letter only to be opened in the event of his death.

Like many families in my position, Simon's memory will continue to be there. It hurts deeply whenever I see his photo, the photo on his wedding day stood proudly outside the Guards Chapel only months before his untimely death. It hurts me to know that he can't see me this day. With me now living in Lancashire it is not that often that I get the opportunity to visit Simon's grave in London – certainly not as often as I would like to. What does make it easier, and for me to be closer to a place of memory to pay my respects, is that his name is inscribed on the Holt war memorial and in St Andrew's church. There is also the tree planted at the National Memorial Arboretum as a permanent reminder. The memorial at Bessbrook Mill, which has now been moved to HQ Northern Ireland at Lisburn, makes a fourth place to visit, which is not too far away, and only a 45-minute flight from Manchester. There is also a plaque erected on the wall inside the Guards Chapel in Wellington Barracks.

A much larger memorial, The Armed Forces Memorial, was officially opened and dedicated by the Queen on 12 October 2007. The memorial had taken seven years to design and build at a cost of £7 million. It is dedicated to the service personnel killed in all conflicts since World War 2. It has the names of over 15,000 people killed and its blank walls have a capacity to add a further 16,000 – a memorial for 'yesterday and tomorrow'. I was privileged to have had some involvement in the consultation phase in the form of a written questionnaire and telephone interviews with the design consultation agency. We were successful in obtaining tickets for the dedication and I was vastly impressed with the huge memorial at The National Memorial Arboretum. The dedication service was attended by the Queen, Prince Philip, Prince Charles and the Prime Minister Gordon Brown. The day culminated in three fly-pasts of military aircraft ranging from years of operational service from World War 2 to the present day.

I felt very comfortable to visit the memorial at Bessbrook as it was where Simon was based, his friends and colleagues placed it there and it remains in the army environment. When I began my research for this book I visited one of the Coldstream Guards websites in August 2002 and was surprised and impressed to read on the message board of all the recent messages in memory of Simon. Dave N was one of them, the man following Simon when the explosion occurred, who regularly visits Simon's grave and has made it clear that he will take anybody to see it should they find it difficult to locate.

I have so many memories of Simon that are etched in my mind, displayed in my house or of those memorials I visit. They may have taken his life but his soul remains alive and strong in the memory of a great friend.

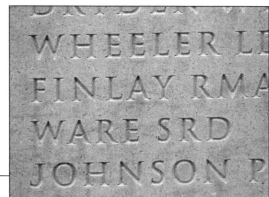

Simon's name engraved on the Armed Forces Memorial.

The impressive Armed Forces Memorial at the National Memorial Arboretum. The names of 16,000 service personnel killed on active service are engraved there, including Simon's.

13

My own return

When my research into this book began, I wrote to the Regimental Sergeant Major of the 1st Battalion Coldstream Guards in December 2002 to arrange a revisit to Northern Ireland so that I could visit the scene of the explosion and Bessbrook Mill for myself and to conduct other inquiries. This would be the first time that I would visit the scene and go to Bessbrook Mill myself. It was during a phone call to Dougie that I mentioned going back to view the scene – Dougie was in front of Simon when the bomb exploded. He told me that the 1st Battalion was in Londonderry until April 2003 and he suggested that I write to the RSM, Ovy. I had met Ovy some years earlier when I visited Simon at Wellington Barracks; he was once Simon's platoon Sergeant or 'Platoon Bloke' as they were referred to in the Guards Division. I knew this would be a great opportunity to pay my respects to Simon and speak to some other soldiers and lay some ghosts to rest.

A few weeks later I got a letter from Johno, the Company Sergeant Major of Number 2 Company, who was once a Lance Corporal with Simon in 14 Platoon in 1991 and he encouraged me to come over to visit the battalion. I spoke to Johno on the phone and he told me to get myself to Belfast and that he would do the rest, so the next day I booked a British Airways flight on the Internet and made my travel plans. Although friends understood that I was doing this as a tribute to Simon, some were not at all too keen for me to go back to Northern Ireland, let alone South Armagh. Once I explained the current terrorist situation, the ceasefire, my intention and reason then they understood.

At 4am on Monday 24 February 2003 on a quiet and wet winter morning I left home and made the short forty-minute journey to Manchester airport for the 7am flight to Belfast City. I was very apprehensive, not just for going back, but to be actually going to South Armagh and to the scene where Simon was killed. I had only viewed the wood from about 200m away in December 1991 and I had always wanted to venture into the wood to see for myself where Simon took his last step so that I could have a picture in my own mind. At that time, in 1991 I wasn't allowed to go any closer than 200 metres from Carrickovaddy Woods as it was out of bounds so soon after Simon's death through fear of similar attacks in close succession. Not only that, but since then I have realised that because it had been used so often before, no soldier dared set foot in it.

The flight was on time landing and I was promptly met in the arrivals lounge by the duty driver from the 2nd Battalion Coldstream Guards for the journey by road to Londonderry. It felt strange to be back in Northern Ireland after ten years but I felt excited and soon after we were on the road from the airport. I noticed a marked police car. I pointed this out to the young guardsman who was driving and he told me that it is how the PSNI operate now, a far cry from what I was used to in 1991. I was used to seeing unmarked armoured Sierra Sapphires and grey armoured Land Rover Hotspurs with grills on the windscreen, guards on the wheel arches and often escorted by army Land Rovers with soldiers riding top cover out of the roof. The changes since 1993 were clear to see compared to the situation when I left Northern Ireland, no doubt they had been influenced by the Peace Talks.

It took about two hours to get to Ebrington Barracks. The driver and escort were two guardsmen who were young in service and therefore would never have known Simon – they weren't even serving in 1991, although they did tell me that they had read about it in the regimental history books. The conversation was varied and a lot was about how the battalion operates now and the current situation in the Province. I found a lot of differences in the way the army now operates in Northern Ireland compared to how it operated years earlier in 1991 and in fact from 1989 when I was in Fermanagh.

My first observation was seeing the two gatemen on duty on the front gate at Ebrington Barracks only wearing berets and although both alert, they were openly in sight of passing motorists and members of the public. We arrived at Ebrington Barracks and were met by Johno at the guardroom and he gave me a warm welcome and took me to my accommodation in the Warrant Officers' and Sergeants' Mess, which I was privileged to be accommodated in. I left the army as a corporal and therefore never benefited from the privilege of life in 'the Sergeants' Mess.' Johno and I then went to the NAAFI for a couple of hours and talked over several brews and discussed our plans for the next two days. We spoke about Simon and the tour and other things in general and I got some good stories to build on. After lunch I was introduced to the Commanding Officer and I told him about the reason for my visit and my book. He suggested that in my spare time in the afternoon I should visit the City walls and sites of Londonderry and in particular 'the Bogside', 'Creggan' and 'Free Derry' corner, which shows the well-known mural of "You are now entering Free Derry" which appears in many books about the history of Northern Ireland, particularly those regarding the early history of the troubles, at the beginning of the 70's and around the time of Bloody Sunday. Although I would like to have done it I declined the offer, and for security and safety reasons I didn't enter the Bogside or the Creggan that day.

The next visit was to Johno's Company Commander to finalise Tuesday's visit to Bessbrook and to confirm the itinerary, route plan, deployment and a security briefing. After evening meal in the Mess I was invited to the bar in the Sergeants' Mess where half a dozen of us had a few beers, and many more, over a good chat. I must say I was made very welcome and was looked after. By the time I got into bed it was just after midnight, with a few beers down my neck – I was up again at 5.30am having not slept too much.

The journey from Ebrington began at 6:15am – Johno, the driver and I in an unmarked car began the journey to Bessbrook Mill. It was still dark and quiet as we began the two-hour journey. We got stuck behind a slow-moving lorry for some distance and the boredom at looking at the back of it and my tiredness got the better of me, so I got an hour's kip on the back seat.

I woke as the car slowed on entering Bessbrook village and noticed it being surrounded by large green corrugated cover-from-view screens supported by large blocks of concrete around the vehicle check point at Bessbrook Mill. They were the familiar surroundings of all the security force bases in Northern Ireland and it certainly brought back many memories of my time being protected by them as I manned observation towers and checked vehicles at permanent vehicle check points. I looked out of the window to see the front main sangar, below which was a large block of local granite engraved with the words 'BESSBROOK MILL'. We were there, and as I looked at my watch it was 8.15am and we

The garden of remembrance at Bessbrook Mill is where many stones of those that did not return are laid. These include LBdr Stephen Restorick and Capt Robert Nairac.

waited to enter the vehicle entrance to the mill as the young soldier on the gate checked and verified who we were. A young Paratrooper stood in combats, his rifle in both hands in the ready position and wearing his coveted red beret, an unusual sight as ten years ago when the threat was somewhat higher in Northern Ireland helmets were worn all the time for our own protection. This was another sign of the changes. Eventually we drove into the Mill and parked up. As Lee, the driver, went to book in at the guardroom, Johno and I went to visit the memorial garden adjacent to the car park. It was a small grassed area with a quantity of well-placed small trees and surrounded on three sides by thick laurel bushes. I observed a number of other memorial stones and trees dedicated to those that had been killed over the years in South Armagh – a small memorial tribute to the many soldiers who, like Simon, had patrolled out of Bessbrook and never returned. There were probably a dozen or so, all laid out in a garden of grass, bushes and trees which looked a peaceful setting. I found Simon's memorial stone nicely placed within a border of large laurel bushes. On a large piece of Irish granite stone was a brass plaque on top of which was engraved a Coldstream Guards cap badge and underneath, the words:

IN MEMORY OF LANCE CORPORAL SRD WARE COLDSTREAM GUARDS KILLED ON ACTIVE SERVICE WITH THE 2ND BATTALION IN NORTHERN IRELAND BORN 23RD JANUARY 1969 DIED 17TH AUGUST 1991
  NULLI SECUNDUS

– the Coldstream Guards motto 'Second to none.' Reality sank in and it suddenly hit me that after hearing of this memorial in 1996 I was finally there to see it for myself.

It was a peaceful private moment as this was the first time I had seen the memorial since it was placed just over seven years earlier and I spent a quiet moment – just Simon's memorial and me – before I placed a Royal British Legion memorial cross at the base of the stone next to another cross placed some time earlier. I still felt vulnerable knowing that South Armagh was always a serious and dangerous threat. Although I was in the compound of a security force base being protected by Paras, I still kept in the back of my mind the terrorist threat. And although I was there for my own personal reasons and for my research, I knew that if the terrorists mounted an attack they would not bother who was hit. Those security measures that were taken over the years in Northern Ireland don't just leave your mind overnight. At this emotional time, those eyes in the back of your head that had worked so tirelessly over the years were still looking out. I then looked at the other tributes in memory of other soldiers killed in South Armagh and I had never seen so many in one small place. I went to Stephen Restorick's memorial, on the far side of the garden and sited on a square piece of granite on which was a bronze plaque in memory of Stephen from his Commanding Officer and all ranks of the Royal Horse Artillery. Planted behind the stone was a cherry tree which no doubt looks nice in full bloom in the summer. I viewed the other memorials; there were many soldiers killed whose names were not all that familiar in the history and public attraction to the troubles in 'Bandit Country,' except one – the memorial to Captain Robert Nairac, (ex-Grenadier Guards), who was killed in May 1977 having been abducted from the *Three Steps Inn*, Crossmaglen and killed whilst on undercover operations. His body has still never been found to this day and he remains one of the 'disappeared'. Captain Nairac had completed many tours of Northern Ireland and in particular spent most of those time in South Armagh operating from Bessbrook Mill. His sole aim was to gain intelligence on PIRA activity to report back so that his intelligence could be used for future operations against the terrorists.

Once finished in the memorial garden we went to meet the Adjutant and then were taken to the intelligence cell for a briefing on the current threat and our planned activity. It was in that room that only 12 years earlier in December 1991 I had gone to start my research. This is where Johno left me in the capable hands of two sergeants from the Parachute Regiment. To respect their privacy and their identity at their request I will refer to them as my 'escorts.' They were two experienced and professional soldiers, who had spent a lot of time studying the terrorist intelligence network in South Armagh. One of them I had met earlier during the start of my research and the other was his work partner; after having met him it seemed like I'd known him ages. They knew why I was there, they knew what I wanted, and they knew they were there to help and knowing my background they both completed their task with maximum efficiency. I was briefed over the plan of action in the way of travel, where we were going and told that the time there was mine and to take as long as I liked, but to be mindful of travel time to Belfast airport to catch the plane back. I was also briefed on any plan of action should anything have occurred. I waited in the car park whilst my escorts drew the weapons and ammunition from the armory.

We jumped into a plain car, all of us were armed, no seat belts on just in case we needed to get out of a sticky situation fast, and having been briefed on the 'actions on.. .' We sped off from the mill and turned right onto the main road towards Cullyhanna. As we turned onto the main road from Bessbrook through the village of Camlough I saw written on a wall in Irish the words 'Oglaighna hEireann', simply meaning 'IRA'. The first town we passed was Belleek and then onto the Newtown Road and south towards the border. Although the situation in Northern Ireland had changed over the years, there was still a threat and there was no time to loiter. There were Irish tricolours and painted yellow, white and green kerbstones everywhere. I could tell that we were deep in a republican anti-security force area – 'Bandit Country.' The journey took about half an hour as we drove the windy roads towards Cullyhanna. We passed several pro-Republican signs, and on a telegraph pole in large wooden letters under each other in white, yellow and green were the letters 'IRA'. Another 'road sign', a white circular board with a red border and a single diagonal red line through the letters 'RUC' indicated that the RUC were prohibited. There was a similar improvised sign, 'Sniper at work.' We continued our journey along the Newtown Road and saw one of the Golf towers, the observation posts erected many years ago to monitor the area, all of which have now been dismantled. We passed a memorial stone on the near side of the road, as we slowed we could see it was dedicated to a 'Republican Volunteer'. We then entered the small village of Belleek, with flying tricolours, and my two escorts pointed out one or two houses and vehicles they recognise as having searched in the past. A memorial play park on the left, known as Francis Hughes Park, was dedicated to another republican victim of the troubles. He was wounded and arrested by the Army after a prolonged manhunt in 1978 and was one of the hunger strikers who protested, and after 51 days he died on 12 May 1981. The journey continued until we came to a junction on the left signposted Cullyhanna. We turned left off the Newtown Road and onto the Carrickovaddy Road and about 150m on the right was Carrickovaddy Wood. There was an open metal swing barrier to the entrance of the wood where the track leads into the wood. I recognised the area, "This is it," I said to my escorts. We stopped the car near to the entrance.

In December 1991 I had patrolled the area and viewed the wood from a distance on the western side from the high ground. The area was familiar. I was about to walk the route that Yankee One Zero Bravo took and the last steps that Simon took on the morning of 17th August 1991 and the last few minutes of his life as a dead man walking unknowing his fate. I had viewed photos of the scene and read many statements from soldiers who took part in the patrol that day and who witnessed the explosion and finally I was there. Over the years I had imagined a picture in my own mind of what the scene would look like but reality was so different as soon as we entered the wood. I imagined a narrow overgrown track, occasionally used by farm vehicles, but in fact it was quite wide and well-used. There was the grass mound that Sammy described in his evidence that he walked on in the middle of the track. The tracks to each side were well-worn by vehicle movement and I began to walk the route of that day with a totally different feeling. The bend in the track was only 30m in and in fact could be seen from the entrance of the wood from Carrickovaddy Road.

The trees were tall and the wood was thick. I entered the bend to the right, and could immediately see where the track then bent to the left and straightened out, as described by Andy and Sammy. This area was fairly open and it was so real! On the right were the remains of rubble from a derelict, which was overgrown, and in fact was not in existence in 1991. I turned left where the track then straightened out, and there I could see it. I stood staring as my heart began to beat faster and my emotions began to take over with the feeling of a lump in my throat. At this point my two escorts told me that they were going to have a look through the wood and would leave me alone for a while. On the right

The scene of the explosion 12 years after Simon was killed. I
stood in the crater on the spot where he died.

As if nothing had happened... Looking towards where Simon approached the contact point.

embankment was a large hole, a large gap where the crater was when the bomb exploded. The embankment was probably 4 foot high but where the crater was there was a big gap. I did not expect to see what I saw let alone any evidence of a bomb crater 12 years later, as I thought that after that long, it would have been overgrown, but I was surprised. It was a personal time for me as I was standing in the spot where my brother was not only killed, but murdered.

Shortly after my visit, on the 18th March 2003, I played a game of golf at Marsden Park Golf Club, Nelson, Lancashire. We'd approached the green on the sixth hole with my ball landing through the green as normal. I walked to the back of the green and placed my trolley next to the next tee box. To my right and at the edge of the green was an overgrown disused bunker. I walked past and had to look twice as it reminded me of the overgrown crater in Carrickovaddy Wood and from then on every time I play that course it reminds me of the scene. I carried on, walking along the track towards the end of the wood, a journey Simon never took. This led me to see where the helicopter pick-up was planned for – only about 200m and he was so close to freedom. I then returned to the crater and began to take in the scene and surrounding trees. There were half-a-dozen uprooted, broken and damaged trees that were in the same position as they were in 1991, although covered in mildew and overgrowth. Out of curiosity I then went into the wood in the direction of where debris was recovered and I took many photos and footage on my camcorder for my own records. I spent a lot of time just looking about the area and walking around to get a feel of what the surviving troops would have been doing whilst running around after the explosion trying to establish some kind of follow-up and search for Simon. It felt strange really, as I did feel some kind of presence in the wood. Maybe it was my mind wanting to feel it or expecting or even hoping that I would and although I do believe in the paranormal, I have never experienced any ghostly phenomena. Even though when I was there, in my own mind I said goodbye – it may have been the feeling of Simon saying goodbye or trying to make contact. Many years ago I read several books about research into the paranormal and ghostly activity and there were two things I picked up on. One of them was that the way ghosts and spirits tend to appear at places and times when they met a violent or painful death. Maybe one day I will revisit Carrickovaddy wood early morning on 17th August, and my presence will not be alone!

One of the escorts found a piece of stone and took his time to etch the words:

LCpl S WARE
1st BN COLDSTREAM GDS
17/08/91
RIP

As an improvised memorial at the scene, I felt this was nice. I then placed it at the edge of the crater in view of the track and placed a Royal British Legion remembrance cross next to it. I thought to myself whether it would remain there for any length of time and if any locals would see it. I know that the majority of people oppose the IRA and the cause but I hope it would remain there, particularly in South Armagh, and who knows, if I make another journey to visit I would hope to see it there. The escort wrote to me in July 2003 to say that he had tasked a patrol to see whether the stone and cross was still there and it was. A later visit noted the delivery of some flowers left at the scene.

I spent about an hour or so at the scene and then began the journey back to Bessbrook to rejoin Johno. I was very glad I made the trip, even after all those years. I would not have been able to return any sooner due to the situation in Northern Ireland. I had closed another chapter in my life and laid some ghosts to rest. I felt that I was closer to Simon and felt he was there and if it were closer to home then I would make the trip more often.

We returned to Bessbrook, had a couple of brews and then Johno and Lee took me back to Belfast airport, a journey of about an hour and a half. I was quiet throughout and just reflecting on what I had just done and I think Johno realised that. I was dropped off at the airport about 1pm, and said my thanks and goodbyes to Johno and Lee as they left and went back to Londonderry.

My plane was not due until 4.05pm so I had a look around the shops. On my outward journey I bought a book at WH Smiths at Manchester airport *The Irish War*. I only tend to find books about 'The Troubles' at airport bookshops. I went into a bookshop at Belfast, which looked well stocked and found the book I had been looking for months – *Death of a Soldier*, by Rita Restorick, the book Rita wrote to dedicate the third anniversary of Stephen's death in February 2000. Needless to say it only took me a short time to read it.

I returned home late on Tuesday 25th February with a feeling of great satisfaction. Not only had it made me write another chapter in my book, but another chapter in my life. At least my remaining friends and relatives can ask me what it was like. It has left my mind with a different perspective and a different image. In a way, I went to say goodbye.

The improvised memorial stone that I placed in the crater
etched by one of my 'escorts' on the revisit.

14

Carol's story

I was Simon's wife at the time of his tragic death and when I was asked to contribute to this book I did not hesitate as I felt it was a wonderful tribute to the life of a wonderful man. It did however conjure up a whirlwind of emotion; to this day there are times that I cry. There are not many days even now that I don't think about Simon. He was my soulmate and the love of my life, so here is my story.

I first met Simon at the end of April/beginning of May 1989. Believe it or not I cannot remember the exact date as I suppose at the time I didn't even consider that this would be the man that I would fall in love with. I used to go drinking with friends in a pub called *The Friend at Hand* in Russell Square, Central London. At the time it was a pub frequented by off-duty police officers and soldiers, and I had in fact only shortly before been involved with a soldier who was in Simon's Company that I had met in the same pub. This relationship, albeit short-term, had not ended very amicably so I wasn't looking to get involved in another. However I spotted Simon standing by the jukebox and he caught my eye. I was later to discover he had seen me and fancied me from afar for a long time and had bided his time knowing that my previous relationship was unlikely to last. I walked over to put some music on and we got talking. We discovered we shared common ground, he came from Enfield, which was familiar to me, as I had come from near that area, and also my dad had come from around that area too. My dad had died some years earlier and Simon too had lost his dad.

We got on so well that I invited him to join my friends and I at the nightclub we were going to, another of our regular haunts called *Hombres*. My friends were less than pleased as they felt getting involved with another squaddie was a bad idea, but it wasn't long before they changed their minds about Simon. Rightly or wrongly we spent the night together and I just knew he was very special. Unfortunately I had plans to travel – I was about to spend three weeks interrailing in Europe only returning home for 3 days before spending the summer working in Majorca with a friend, so I said goodbye but took his address and promised to write, which I did. I sent a postcard and told him to meet me in the *Friend at Hand* pub on my return before I headed off again. I was amazed when I walked into the pub to see him standing at the bar on the exact date and time that I had asked him to – if I had known the type of person he was I would never have doubted it. I knew then that this was the man I wanted to spend my life with. We spent another night together and then I had to say goodbye again, but we kept in touch with letters and postcards. I returned home in late August not to London but home to my mum and step-dad in Hertfordshire, so we were only able to talk on the phone, which we did often.

Simon came to my hometown to see me and to meet my parents. My mum was her usual friendly self but even though Simon was charming and polite my step-dad was very reserved. He was known to be a bit of a snob and despite having been in the army himself I think he felt I should be involved with someone 'better'. To make matters worse whilst at home I made a visit to the doctors where I discovered I was pregnant. Although I suspected

Simon and Carol's second date. The happy couple.

as much I was distressed to have my suspicions confirmed, as it was not something I had planned. My mum was very upset and furious with me for being so stupid – although I thought I had been careful, obviously not careful enough. My step-dad refused to even speak to me and was certainly not prepared to welcome Simon into the family seeing him as the perpetrator of a 'crime' against me. So a huge rift was caused and this was before I had even broken the news to Simon, which I was dreading – I had no idea how he would feel. I remember meeting Simon at the station and going to the local pub where we should have been having a good time, but all the time I was thinking about the news I was going to have to tell him. Simon walked me home and we sat on a park bench where I told him the news. This was the first time Simon told me that he loved me and I already knew that I loved him too; he told me that he would stick by me whatever decision I made. He then had to break the news to his mum whose reaction could not have been more different. She was cross that he had been stupid but he told her that he loved me and her reply was "well you better make sure you take care of her then."

Sadly I took the decision to end the pregnancy as I had no job and was living back at home and it wasn't the right time to have a baby. I know that many people will think I was wrong and as I had always wanted children it was not a decision taken lightly. I was heartbroken and knew that I would live with my decision forever. My doctor at home had refused to refer me on the grounds of his religion so I was seen by my doctor in London, who was very kind and understanding and referred me to a London hospital. This meant spending the night before in London with a friend who gave up her bed for us where we spent a sleepless night. I was worried and upset and Simon was a constant comfort and support, trying not to show me that he was upset too. The next day I was accompanied to the hospital by Simon and my two close friends, Rhiannon and Lindsey, who all stayed with me up until the last moment. This was to be a turning point for my friends in their relationship with Simon, as they stayed with him all day whilst he worried constantly until he knew I was all right. They could see how much he loved and cared for me and this made him special to them, too. I went home the next day and my mum was wonderful but my step-dad still refused to speak to me.

The following weekend I was traveling to Norfolk with Simon and his brother to meet his parents. I was a nervous wreck, unsure how they would feel about me under the circumstances, but I needn't have worried as they couldn't have been nicer and more welcoming. I was pampered and looked after all weekend and returned home to a completely different scenario. The rift between my step-dad and me was as bad as ever and it made it impossible for me to live at home and continue our relationship. I decided to move into a flat with my two friends in Shepherd's Bush and the relationship between Simon and I got better and better.

We were to be separated yet again when Simon went on exercise to Kenya for 6 weeks and this was my first realisation of what life was like with a soldier. We had no phone so had to rely on letters all the time. It was awful, I missed him so much and couldn't wait for him to come back. It's true what they say as absence really does make the heart grow fonder and I just loved him even more.

Life was good, we were both working and had enough money to go out and have a good time, which we did. It was sad that my mum and step-dad couldn't see how happy we were. My brother David was a saving grace as he always supported Simon and admired him for having the guts to stand up and say how much he loved me and wouldn't hurt me, and we had the support of Simon's family too. It wasn't all bad, even my mum came round and used to talk to Simon on the phone and was convinced that my stepfather would come round eventually. Simon was still not welcome at home because of my step-dad's attitude, so when I visited mum Simon used to go fishing on the canal. Mum would always pack me off with a 'goodie bag' for him as she felt bad about the way things were.

We spent Christmas 1989 with Simon's mum and step-dad and brother in Norfolk and had a fantastic time. I was expected to spend the New Year at home with my parents but without Simon, which I knew would be difficult, so the eve of New Year's Eve we all went nightclubbing to have our own celebration. On the way up the steps to leave the club Simon grabbed my hand and suddenly blurted out "will you marry me?" I was stunned as it was totally unexpected but I said yes straight away and then found out that all my friends were in on it. He brought me a beautiful amethyst and diamond ring and we set a date for March 9th 1991.

We worked hard and saved constantly, Simon did extra security work and I worked nights. I was a qualified nurse and worked at Charring Cross hospital for a local nursing agency, which paid reasonably well.

My mum had promised us the money to pay for our reception and we were saving the rest – sadly mum wasn't to be there to see us marry as after battling against ovarian cancer she sadly died in July 1990, and once again we faced difficult times together. Simon's love never faltered – he was always there to support me. We had planned a holiday to Turkey, as we knew we wouldn't be able to afford to go on holiday for some time but I felt guilty about going as my mum had just died. Mum had traveled to Turkey and had given us books and information and told us places to visit so I felt I owed it to her. So we went and despite the sadness we had a fantastic two weeks, which now I will be forever grateful for.

We came home and continued saving hard, fortunately my stepfather honoured my mum's promise to pay for the reception, which made things a little easier. Things changed at home as one of my friends decided to move out of the flat to share with another friend, so Simon got permission from the army to live out of barracks and moved in to make it

Simon and Carol's wedding day 9th March 1991. Simon deployed
to Northern Ireland two days later and never returned.

up to three again, and despite the old saying of 'two's company three is a crowd' we all
got on well together and it meant we could share more of our lives.

Simon was always a great support to one of our flat mates when she suffered an
emotional break-up with her long-term boyfriend. Simon was very kind, caring and tolerant
towards her, never moaning even though it sometimes got us down and I wasn't always
tolerant. Living together meant we could work harder towards our wedding. Christmas
1990 was our first alone together and a brief respite before the wedding plans really escalated.

Our wedding day was everything I had hoped for. We were married in the Guards
Chapel, Wellington Barracks, me in my fabulous dress and Simon stunningly good-looking
in his Coldstream Guards red tunic; my stepfather even gave me away. I remember every
moment of that day from waking up to going to bed and was having such a good time
at our reception that we did not want to leave.

A few months before our wedding we found out that Simon's battalion were being posted to Germany for 5 years. I had just started a new job and was happy and settled so I did not want to go and neither did Simon, so he applied to transfer to the 2nd Battalion. We soon found out that the 1st Battalion were going to the Gulf War so I breathed a huge sigh of relief that Simon would not be going, only to find out that he would be going to Northern Ireland for 6 months leaving on the 11th March – only two days after our wedding. I had to accept that this was life as an army wife. We spent the weekend of the wedding buying things for our new married quarter to make it homely.

On the evening Monday 11th March I had to watch Simon walk down the stairs and out of my life for however many weeks until he was back home on leave. I had no choice but to get on with things and tried not to think about the dangerous place he was in. I soon got to know some of the other wives – Karen whose husband was in the Gulf, and Sheila whose husband was serving in Northern Ireland with Simon. We shared meals together; the flats were a trail of telephone extension wires, as we never left our flats without the phone just in case our husbands phoned. You always knew who was where by where the wires went; it was like having another family always there to support you.

The families' officer, Keith, arranged days out for us, one of which was to visit the Guards training depot at Pirbright, Surrey. We all attempted the assault course followed by a barbeque – it was a huge morale booster and great fun and by coincidence I met a girl that I knew from my nurse training.

Our next trip was a day trip to France on Saturday 17th August, a date that will be forever etched in my memory. When I recall things now I remember speaking to Simon on the Wednesday night, when he told me he would be going on an operation until the Saturday and so he wouldn't be able to talk to me until he returned. When we said our goodbyes it was the usual "I love you's" but this night he added something extra that I've never forgotten. He just said, "remember I will always love you". It did not seem significant at the time but now I will never forget it.

We all had a great day out in France drinking and eating, shopped 'till we dropped in the hypermarket, loaded the coach up with tons of booze and cigarettes and settled onto the ferry for the journey home. We continued drinking and having a laugh but during the journey the families' officer disappeared with the coach driver and was gone for some time. He came back and acted as if nothing was untoward, making some excuse about a problem with the coach driver. I found out later that he had in fact just been told the news that Simon had been killed but he couldn't say anything because there were people awaiting our return to Dover to break the news as it would not be appropriate to tell me in the middle of the English Channel. How he managed the rest of the journey I will never know. It's strange but despite the significance of that tragic day I cannot remember the time scale. I know that we arrived in Dover in the evening but I don't recall the time. I remember my friend Sheila being ushered off the coach by the families' officer and he asked her how well she knew me. Well, she hadn't known me very long, which is what she said, she became suspicious and asked what was going on. Keith was worried about telling her as she was five months pregnant, but after assuring him that she was all right he told her that something awful had happened and that he needed to get me off the coach with the minimum of fuss, which she did. I don't know if she knew how awful the news was but I think she probably guessed.

I stepped down from the coach and Keith took me by the arm and told me I needed to come with him. I then saw a man in a suit flanked by two female police officers walking towards me. People say they have a sixth sense at these times and already know what they are about to be told but I didn't. I had spent four and a half months putting any ideas of death or injury to the back of my mind, so when I saw these people walking towards me I thought I was about to be arrested. I thought I must have overdone the amount of booze and cigarettes I had brought back but everyone else had brought as much as I had so why had I been singled out?

I was led into a small room and sat on a bench seat, which resembled a changing room or toilet. Then this suited man introduced himself as the Regimental Adjutant, whatever that meant; if he had told me his name I could not remember. He then broke the news to me that "Simon had been killed this morning in an IRA landmine explosion". He also told me it was very quick and he would never have known anything about it. If this was meant to comfort me it didn't, all I remember was screaming. I've never screamed in my life except on fun fair rides and this was certainly no comparison. The Adjutant sat on the floor with his head in his hands, the two police officers were in tears and I just broke down looking at this young man in total disbelief, who didn't know what else to say. I don't think he had ever done anything like this before and I almost felt sorry for him. Somebody got me a cup of sweet tea and I remember thinking "this is disgusting, I don't take sugar". Sheila didn't know what to say or do so she asked Keith to get Liz from the coach. Liz and I had trained together as nurses and she thought she would be able to help, she was from Northern Ireland herself and tried to comfort me but all she could do was to shout and swear about the bastard IRA, amongst other expletives. We obviously could not stay in this room forever so Keith instructed my friends to get my things off the coach as the adjutant was taking me to my brother's house. My friends Karen and Sheila were coming in the car with me. When they went back on the coach all the wives were asking what was going on and Sheila just told them it was bad news, which confirmed what they already suspected. You can imagine how shocked they were and they had to face the journey home knowing that one of us had lost their husband.

I remember stopping at a motorway service station en route and by unfortunate coincidence the coach with the wives also stopped. I sat there feeling like a goldfish in a bowl. I was taken to my brother's house in Hertford and I don't remember much more about that night. I sat in a state of shock in the living room hearing the whispers of the adjutant talking to my brother in the hallway. He explained to my brother that I would not be able to see Simon's body due to the nature of his death and that he was to dissuade me if I asked. My brother assured him that I wasn't stupid and I was aware of the nature of his death so would be unlikely to ask. I went to bed but didn't sleep; I got up early and sat watching the news on television. A reporter stood talking about the soldier killed in Northern Ireland, and that he had been named as Lance Corporal Simon Ware, a married man from London. The reporter was stood in front of a large hole in the ground and I remember thinking, "that's my husband your talking about and that's where he once stood", but it did not seem real. It couldn't be my husband he was talking about, not my Simon. My brother took me home, I don't remember the journey or any conversation, I remember stopping at a garage for a drink and I remember walking into our flat where we had spent so little time together – exactly 9 days in total, 2 days after our wedding and 7 days in May when he came home on leave. I recall the day he went back to Northern

Ireland after being on leave, he stood at the bedroom door looking at me lying in bed. We had already said our goodbyes and when he stood at the bedroom door I remember telling him to just go as the longer he stayed there the worse it would be. I didn't know then that it would be the last time I would see him, perhaps if I had known I would have held on to that moment a bit longer. Would it have made it any better? I doubt it.

I walked into what should have been our home – it seemed emptier than ever and I remember Karen's husband Dave rushing down the hallway and just hugging me. He didn't say anything, he didn't need to. He had been in the Gulf and he was safe, as were other mates of Simon from the 1st Battalion. I can't imagine how they must have felt, they had been in a war but they were OK but Simon wasn't. Keith revisited later that same day and went through some formalities with me which were difficult to take in but over the next few weeks he was to be constantly by my side and keeping my spirits up, but offering sympathy when I cried. I would never have coped without him, or the stream of friends that constantly came by coaxing me to eat even though I didn't want to. We drank all the cheap French booze, smoked all the cigarettes and talked about Simon constantly. They shared my memories and songs that reminded me of him.

The next hurdle was the return of Simon's body to English soil. He was being flown back to Heathrow and Keith had arranged for me to meet his homecoming. I remember the journey to Heathrow but I don't recall who was with me. I remember the kindness of the people at the airport; they showed us to a comfortable room and offered us tea. We waited there for the plane to land and clearance to be given for us to go onto the tarmac. I recall standing on the tarmac and remember the Commanding Officer's wife and Keith and his wife being there. I remember Keith's wife, Sandra, squeezing my hand and telling me how brave I was, but I didn't feel very brave I just felt grief-stricken. Simon's brother, mother and stepfather were also there but I don't remember. It was as if I was so consumed by my own grief that I couldn't take on board anyone else's. I recall seeing the coffin appear at the top of the steps to the hold of the plane and a union flag being draped over it. It hit me then that he was home but he was dead – pallbearers marched his coffin the short distance to a waiting hearse. Keith led me over, where I said my goodbyes and placed a red rose on top of the coffin and told him how much I loved him.

During that week a memorial service was held at the sea cadet unit I belonged to in Harrow and was conducted beautifully by the Padre. Seeing the sea cadet ensign lowered to half-mast brought home to those young cadets the reality of violence, war and the keeping the peace. The ensign remained lowered all week. I knew that Simon would want a military funeral and the families' officer had noted my requests.

The funeral was held at the Guards Chapel, Wellington Barracks on the 23rd August, only 6 days after his death and five months after we had exchanged our wedding vows in the same chapel. I had been informed that there were likely to be press and TV cameras at the chapel when I arrived, but nothing prepared me when the car pulled up at the steps and I saw the mass of photographers and cameras. There may not have been that many but to me it seemed like hordes. I had to try and compose myself before getting out of the car – these people were intruding into my grief, and I was completely taken aback. Simon was not a celebrity, he was my husband and he was killed doing the job he loved. I sound as if I am angry with them but the truth is that afterwards I was grateful. The media was sensitive in their reporting, they paid tribute to a young man who did not deserve to die and I have kept just about every press cutting as part of my memorial to him, which I will keep forever.

I was also astounded when I walked into the chapel to see not a single pew empty, a sea of soldiers all coming to pay their own personal respects. At the top where we had stood on our wedding day was his coffin draped in the union flag with his forage cap, belt and Northern Ireland medal together with the same rose I had placed there only a few days before. I held another rose throughout the service ready for his burial. Nothing prepares you for this sight. My mum had only died the year before, she was my best friend but here was my other best friend, my soulmate and I had come to say goodbye. We sang, amongst others, a hymn that we sang on our wedding *Thine be the glory*; it had reminded Simon of his dad, who had passed away before we met. How appropriate – I know it is about the glory of God, but my Simon was glorious. Following the service, there was a long journey across central London to Lavender Hill Cemetery in Enfield where he was to be buried. The journey seemed endless, staring at the hearse in front of us. We had a convoy behind us of minibuses and a coach; I think several times we were escorted through red lights in order to keep the convoy together.

We stood around the grave where Simon was being buried next to his dad. I don't recall any of the words that were said as I only remember the tight grip I had on my wreath, so tight that the middle section nearly fell out. Then the Last Post was played and even now my eyes fill up every remembrance Sunday when I hear it played. I threw photos of our wedding into the grave along with his Arsenal scarf and my rose; this was my final goodbye. I was touched to see a member of the RUC there to pay his respects on their behalf, also a couple we had made friends with in Turkey and police officers in uniform, not there on official duties but friends of mine who had liked and respected Simon and had come to offer their support.

Then followed the wake, a wake that was unlike any other I had been to. It sounds disrespectful but we played drinking games – after all Simon was only 22 when he died and was vibrant and fun-loving and it seemed fitting that we celebrated his life – time for mourning and crying could come later.

Simon's mum, Lesley, spent the following week with me; she needed to be with the person he had spent his time with, to share the memories with me. I loved her, she was a wonderful woman but now I wanted to be on my own and couldn't cope with another person's grief. She had lost her son and I can't imagine how that must have felt but I had lost my husband and I was selfish and wanted time to grieve alone and I felt frustrated by her presence, though I would never have told her so. We wanted to visit the Guards Chapel and have time in there without the glare of others, so we had a daytrip, only to find it closed. All the anger and frustration come out and I banged on the door not believing we couldn't get in, I sat on the steps and cried. I was inconsolable; this was a special place that held both happy and sad memories. Simon's stepfather, Terry, came to London to take Lesley home and along with my two close friends, Rhiannon and Lindsey, we went back to the cemetery to visit his grave. It was one huge mass of flowers and I was totally overcome by the sight, it was so beautiful in a sea of sadness.

Lesley returned home and gradually life returned to a semblance of normality. I went back to work and took things one day at a time, there was still so much to deal with in the near future but the worse part was over. I had constant support from Keith who helped me with financial matters and discovered that Simon had taken out a life insurance policy while he was serving in Northern Ireland. Part of me thinks maybe somehow he knew he wouldn't come home but one way or the other he wanted to make sure I was cared for.

I have spoken to friends and family involved at the time and often wondered why I was taken back to my brother's on the night Simon was killed. How come they already knew and how could the army have known that my brother would now be my next of kin? I soon discovered that my sister-in-law had heard the news on the television that morning but no name had been given. She has a peculiar ESP and although she is not a negative person, when she heard the news she had a strong feeling that it was Simon. She doesn't know why but recalls feeling so convinced that she phoned my brother at work and told him what she felt; he obviously tried to reassure her by saying that there were so many soldiers out there that it could be any one of them. So she continued to listen to news reports, which still did not name the soldier who had been killed. She also knew that I was in France and as next-of-kin I would need to be informed before the name could be released, which made her more convinced. She spoke to my brother again who suggested she phoned one of the TV companies to try and get information, which she did. Finally getting through to the MOD and after going through a series of questions to confirm her relationship to me they were finally prepared to tell her that she was right. The man she spoke to asked where I should be taken once I had been informed. She naturally felt that I should come to my brother's; she then had the grim task of telling my brother the tragic news she felt from the start.

Other friends knew he had died but I had no idea how they knew or who had told them, as I didn't recall telling anyone so someone must have done it for me. Whoever did I am grateful as I didn't think I could have faced that task.

I was not involved in much more of the aftermath other than my own grief. I know that an inquest was held many months after his death which I couldn't face going to. I also could not face reading the inquest report or post-mortem report for many years after, though I have done now. It makes grim reading so I am glad I did not read it at the time.

Even now his memory still lives on in the hearts and minds of friends and family. My brother and sister-in-law have a photo of Simon taken on our wedding day holding my nephew (now 16) in his arms. He was a pageboy in a replica uniform, they had a plaque engraved and placed at the bottom of the photo. My sister-in-law says they will never put it away and it has been the first picture on the wall in every house they've been in since his death; I think she sees him as a guardian angel looking over them.

Simon spent only two years in my life and despite some of the tragedies we went through I always remember my time with him as happy and fun and full of laughter. We used to love spending Sunday afternoons with friends in the local pub then going home and getting even more drunk and watching videos. When we went out to parties he was always joining in with the singing, dancing and general larking about and would never sit watching from the sideline. A couple of amusing memories are of Simon prancing about in the living room wearing an adult all-in-one sleep suit that belonged to me – he looked liked an overgrown baby and my friend has the photographic evidence to prove it! He did look like a daft prat.

I also remember him running into the flat during the summer of 1990, out of breath, stood in bare feet holding his flip-flops in his hand. He looked a sorry state and this supposedly-fit soldier looked like he was about to breath his last and could barely get a word out. It turned out he had been chased all the way up Shepherd's Bush Road by a Rottweiler. My friend and I nearly wet ourselves laughing, what a sight this must have been!

We had a great relationship and have sometimes heard couples say how good theirs is and that they never argue. The cynical amongst us would say "yeah right, who are they trying to kid?" but I have to say that in our two years together we only ever had two arguments, both of which are now funny. Simon had never let me down but one argument was caused by the one and only time that he did. We were meant to be going to a Trafalgar Night dinner with the sea cadet unit I was involved with and he knew he was meant to be home in time to get ready and drive across London to Harrow but I didn't know where he had gone. I worried and waited, I was seriously worried he was laying in a hospital somewhere. I phoned my brother to say that we might be late and why, he just laughed and said, "don't worry, he'll be drunk somewhere with his mates". I said there was no way Simon would do that to me but I did phone the *Duke of York* pub in Victoria where I knew he sometimes drank, to see if he was meeting his army mates. They said he wasn't there – but he was! Sometime after getting the phone book out ready to phone around the hospitals I then looked out of the window to see him staggering up the road very much the worse for drink; he had apparently momentarily lost consciousness in the gutter whilst waiting for a bus home from the tube station. He came to and staggered home to the worst tongue lashing of his life, I accused him of not loving me because if he did then he wouldn't have let me down; his face said it all, and he was devastated that I could even think that. He got ready in double-quick time and although he was meant to be navigating he spent the entire journey with his head out of the window in case he was sick in my friend's car. By the time we got there he had recovered enough to enjoy the evening, though he drank orange juice all night. Everyone thought it was hysterically funny and I must admit it did not take me long to forgive him.

The only other argument we had was another funny one in hindsight. Simon had been working extra hours doing security work to save for our wedding so he was tired. He came home one evening and fell asleep on the floor. I was cooking dinner before going on my night shift and had left him to sleep but expected him to wake up when it was ready to eat. I shouted out to him that dinner was ready and to wake up but he didn't so I went over and shook him. I even nudged him hard with my foot but got nothing more than grunts. Eventually I said that if he didn't wake up I would throw his dinner on him. He still didn't wake up so I dropped a plate of sausage casserole, peas and mash all over him. The most infuriating thing was that he continued to lay there and just brushed the dinner off with his hand. It wasn't until I sat down and cried that he got up and said he was sorry and he hadn't meant to upset me. The next thing we were in fits of laughter, he couldn't believe what I'd done and I couldn't believe I'd done it.

I have regrets since his death. The most significant one is ending my pregnancy, which would have meant Simon living on in another person, although the child would never have known his father; maybe it was for the best. We had planned to start a family as soon as he came back from Northern Ireland. Another regret plagued me for a long time after – would Simon have been alive today if I had gone to Germany with him? Did he change battalions to make me happy? Or was it what he wanted to do? He told me he didn't want to go but he always put me first so I will never know, maybe this was his fate. They say only the good die young and whoever 'they' are, where Simon was concerned, they weren't wrong.

There are lots of happy and sad memories and Simon will forever live on in my heart and mind. I believe I am lucky to have found my soulmate – not many people do. He understood me and loved and cared for me like no other man ever has. Time is a great healer. You never get over the death of someone you love but you do learn to live with it and move on with life. I have never been happy since but I did marry again, and although unsuccessful, I have a beautiful daughter who provides me with the happiness I need, and who knows, I may meet someone else in the future to share my life with ... but I'll never forget Simon.

This is the end of the story of my part in Simon's life. It may be too late now but I would like to add my thanks to all those who were there for me during this traumatic time. I hope they know how grateful I was for their support and also to the communities in Northern Ireland who took the time to write me and offer their sympathy and words of comfort – it was much appreciated. I never wrote back at the time as I was inundated by so many letters but just felt unable to put pen to paper at the time, and after a while it seemed too late to do so.

15

Conclusion

My determination from the moment of Simon's death was to investigate, enquire and find out as many facts, rumour, gossip and speculation as I could about the circumstances surrounding his murder and ascertain what was fact and what wasn't. I suppose for years I had let it lie as I continued in my army career and life thinking that what had been done by other agencies was all that could have been done.

On 27th September 2002 I formed part of the on-call firearms response team during the Labour Party Conference at Blackpool. I was based at police headquarters at Preston for eight days and had some time on my hands. I sat in the target control room of the indoor range and began writing the memorial chapter to this book, which was the beginning of many chapters to follow. I found it hard to believe that by the time I began to write this final concluding chapter, I was in fact really making a final end to a long investigation into the circumstances and speculation surrounding Simon's death, and in fact summarising the final part of his life.

The target control room of the indoor shooting range at Police
Headquarters. It was in this small room that this whole story began.

In the two years following the explosion, and whilst I was still serving in the Army I went out of my way to find out what had happened. By the time I had attended the inquest I was of the naive belief that it was the end of it and that all the information and facts were 'out in the open' with all questions answered, but felt I was wrong. By the summer of 2002, when the memorial dedication had taken place and Simon's name was engraved on the Holt War Memorial, I felt that it was time I worked on a project of a lasting memory and a personal achievement. It was about this time that I watched a documentary on television called *The Real Bravo Two Zero* and a few weeks later I read the book of the same title. Written by Michael Asher, it was his story about revisiting Iraq ten years after Andy McNab led the SAS patrol, Bravo Two Zero, behind Iraqi lines to locate and destroy Scud missiles during the first Gulf War of 1991. Michael Asher was conducting his own investigation into exactly what happened and I thought that if he could travel to Iraq ten years after to conduct an investigation then I'm sure I could travel to Northern Ireland twelve years after Simon was killed to conduct my own investigation too.

I decided to embark on writing this book, as a personal goal in memory of Simon and really as to what happened, what I knew and how I felt and to share my story. For years I looked back on how saddened I was to lose my brother, who was a good friend and a large part of my life. I wanted to let it be known what terrorism can do to someone who was just doing the job they are trained to do, and a job he enjoyed. Also, to describe what effect it had on the life of a family losing out on the things that we can't now do.

By this time I was an investigative police officer and my mind was more inquisitive. I began to probe a lot more and to network my enquiries to speak to many people. Over the time I realised there were many unanswered questions and a few stones left unturned and in a way I became surprised, pleased and at times disappointed with what I discovered.

Since September 2002 I had received a lot of encouragement from family and friends when they learned that I was writing this book. A lot of this support was from members of both battalions of the Coldstream Guards, who wrote to me expressing an interest in what I was doing and who were equally keen to find things out. Many of them commented on how brave they thought I was and thought it was a tremendous effort to achieve and I took comfort from their support, many of whom I had never met. In all, they gave me the motivation to persevere. There were times during my writing when I had to stop when things got too emotional, and I would have to put the pen down and then come back to it some time later, but it was the strength and the encouragement and my determination that made me continue.

Over the years I came across several points of interest which I felt had a contributing factor to Simon's death. Not all of them had sufficient evidence to prove it, but the circumstances and the 'gut feeling' gave reasonable grounds to suggest that they could have contributed to his death. I would never have expected either the Army or the police to confirm these speculations, but they arose for a reason. They were not only issues that I had found, but they were ones that I was told by several people and confirmed by others. I had raised them with the relevant agencies at the time but as you will read on, I never got many full explanations.

The history of the Troubles had been plagued with speculation over many murders, with questions never being fully answered. I will leave it to the reader to weigh up the 'balance of probabilities'. And in no specific order I will draw your attention to the issue of a montage of photographs, a set of 96 photographs of known terrorists that went missing.

Commanders of all levels in Northern Ireland are all issued with various collections of pocket-size photographs of known terrorists that frequent their 'patch', or area of responsibility. They are an *aide mémoire* that you can easily refer to if you see a known terrorist suspect and need to doublecheck that person's identity. The montage will have brief details of the suspect's date of birth, address and details of vehicles they use and their associates, which can be used to confirm their sighting for intelligence gathering. On one occasion Simon told me that somehow a set of photos had been lost by somebody whilst on patrol. This story was reported in a national newspaper following Simon's death and also in a book that details the circumstances relating to every terrorist related death during the Troubles. Now when patrols deploy, individuals are issued with specific pieces of equipment and other items that may assist in the task and it is the responsibility of that individual to make sure they don't lose those items. It is also the responsibility of the commander to regularly check that individuals still have possession of that kit before, during and after every patrol. Simon told me that on more than one occasion patrols had been sent out to search the area where it was believed the photos were lost. This would turn out to be manpower-intensive, especially if the montage was found, as it would need to be cleared and made safe by the ATO before it would be recovered. The terrorists had the ability to booby trap attractive items that they thought soldiers may pick up whilst on patrol and it was part of your training to avoid touching such items. It would have been all too easy for the terrorists to booby trap a set of montages so as to kill or injure a soldier should it be picked up. Those montages, to my knowledge were never found. Though Simon had not told me that they had been found, and the MoD had failed to admit the loss, it was reported in a national newspaper following Simon's death, that "locals said the army had been combing the area intensively since the Security Forces admitted secret reports of 96 IRA suspects had been lost ten days ago." Patrols had been deployed to a specific area to comb and look for the photographs. Terrorist observers, or 'dickers' as they are called, would have noticed the intense army patrols in one area and possibly set up a device so as to ambush future patrols. After all, terrorists are highly motivated individuals, and don't just place bombs in the middle of nowhere in the hope of them going off. A number of Simon's colleagues in Number 4 Company at the time and still serving, at the time of my research, are adamant that a pattern was set and that the IRA had identified it.

Another thought... As a commander it was all too easy to choose an easy quicker route from A to B, but when you are dealing with a terrorist threat you have to sacrifice the easy way out and go out of your way to complete the task safely, even if it means getting cold and wet over some hard ground. In July 1991 the body of Thomas Oliver was dumped in a lay-by near to the junction of the Newtown Road and Carrickovaddy Road. Thomas had been shot by the IRA with a .38 revolver after having been discovered that he was a 'tout' who had supplied information to the Garda. A joint RUC and army search and clearance operation took place to ensure that Thomas Oliver's body was not booby-trapped before his removal. This would have been a time where both static and mobile army and RUC patrols would be deployed. The location of Oliver's body was just 500 hundred metres from Carrickovaddy Wood. One patrol commander of a satellite call sign involved in the recovery of Thomas Oliver's body told me that whilst tasked to patrol a specific area, he patrolled through open boggy fields to the north of the Carrickovaddy Wood to some high ground west of the wood which he found difficult to negotiate. He had actually patrolled to the high ground that I had described earlier as dominating during my visit to the wood in December 1991, the high ground that I had looked over towards Carrickovaddy Wood. Once on the high ground he could see Carrickovaddy Wood and thought how easy it would be to patrol the shorter and drier route towards the wood through the dry field or the easy road to the south. Using his professional patrol skills he decided that although it was boggy and longer, it would be safer to retrace his route north of the wood. Some four weeks after the clearance of the body of Thomas Oliver, Simon was killed. It was felt that maybe the device that killed Simon could have been planted as a secondary device in the IRA's hope that patrolling troops securing the cordon for the Thomas Oliver incident may have been hit. After all, Carrickovaddy Wood is only a few hundred metres from where Thomas Oliver's body was left and would have been a welcoming piece of shelter, out of view, for a patrolling call sign to pop in for a rest, brew or fag break.

The reasons why the terrorists chose that particular spot to site a Victim Operated IED are obscure but it is possible that it was linked with the murder of Thomas Oliver whose body was discovered 500 metres to the north-east of Carrickovaddy Wood on the 19th July 1991. The device may have been sited to catch the cordon or satellite patrols in the connected clearance operation. Whatever the reason, it was a well-sited IED in a natural choke-point in a wood that the army had probably been using for the last 20 years and had left compo ration tins and rubbish to confirm this. This ensured the enemy was aware of the army presence over time. Although victim-operated, the precise method of initiation is yet to be confirmed.

Having spoken to many people during my research a handful had made some indirect comments about certain standards, or lack of them. There were soldiers who mentioned things briefly but stopped themselves from elaborating. It was as if they did not want to point the finger at anyone, but wanted to let me know. One of them wrote a detailed letter to me and ended it with the following: "I have heard many stories from individuals involved both directly and indirectly into the hows and whys of what occurred that morning, however this would be second-hand information to you. I am sure that you will benefit from the individuals themselves."

Many people who had a big input and involvement in that patrol declined to comment or contact me during my research. Now, if you have nothing to hide then why not speak out? This made me wonder if they were hiding something. There were many who were involved on that day who never replied to my letters. It may have been that over the years they had moved on, some even declined to help after I had spoken to and e-mailed them; on the other hand they may not have wanted to remind themselves of that horrible day, and who could blame them? Many of them no doubt have recurring memories, either good or bad, that still trouble them to this day, and I respect that. One told me that there were an enormous amount of mixed gut feelings – "hatred, vengeance, anger, waste, what are we doing here, sitting ducks and round up all the terrorists and shoot them". Another went onto say " I still think of what happened that day, not too often, but now and again and it's always that hole in the ground and those colours that I don't think I will ever forget." Similarly someone contacted me concerned that there were so many unanswered questions about Simon's murder, and hoped that the book would answer them.

As mentioned previously, Simon was full of "you just know" quotes. One in particular was "you just know if anyone's going to get wasted on this tour, its gonna be me; just my fucking luck that would be." It was felt that Simon had said that for a reason. Maybe he predicted his own death or maybe he had felt that things were not right, but we will never know.

A summarising note on the serious incident report mentions that the siting of the device was based on the fact that patrols had visited the wood before, in fact three times by Number One Company based at Newtownhamilton since March 1991, and that it would almost certainly be visited again within a six to twelve month period. The wood is one of many natural features that are attractive to patrols for patrol tasks and searches. Sammy stated that he had used the wood only a couple of weeks before the explosion. A further significant factor which is of note too is in that on the 20th February 1990, a helicopter chase took place following suspicious activity near to Carrickovaddy Wood, which made the wood a logical place for routine searches, therefore attracting troops to search and following patterns that were set it enabled the terrorists to plan an attack from the wood.

The activation method of the device still remains a sensitive subject. In fact one of my lines of enquiry led me to contact the bomb disposal team at Bessbrook to view their report, to be told that it remains at a 'Secret' level for 30 years, as the army is still developing tactics and equipment to counteract further similar devices. This surprised me somewhat, that twelve years down the line the army were still trying to counteract it in this time of modern technology. Having exhausted my enquiries I was left with the last resort of writing a detailed report to the Ministry of Defence in an effort to answer my questions, doubts and speculation. After all, if I could not get the answers from those involved then I had to ask the people in charge.

My research shortly after Simon's death revealed that some time before the 2nd Battalion Coldstream Guards arrived in South Armagh an item of electrical ECM equipment was lost by a previous regiment. This item comes in various forms – several are carried on every patrol to assist in the task and safety of the patrol to prevent a specific terrorist attack from radio-controlled IED's. That is it explained briefly as it remains a sensitive issue which can't be elaborated on. Further indications suggest that this item of equipment landed in the hands of the IRA who soon ascertained what it was used for. A power unit was then constructed in such a way that the mode of initiation was compatible with how the piece of electrical equipment worked. This power unit was attached to a 250lb landmine that was then dug into an embankment on the eastern side of a track that led through Carrickovaddy Woods, so much so that it would cause maximum effect. This was a wood the IRA knew the army had used on occasions recently, possibly in conjunction with the body of Thomas Oliver, and knowing that they would probably use it again. It's simple when you look at it – an item of electrical kit and a collection of terrorist photos are lost, the IRA get hold of it and work out how it operates, they then plant a bomb in the area where it was lost, knowing that patrols would be using that equipment in that area. They then deliberately place the body of a murdered tout nearby hoping that this will attract patrols in the area. Not only that, but they planted it in a wood which has been used many times before and know that it will be used again by troops carrying the same piece of equipment. Their methods are twofold in that if it does not work for one then it may work for the other. What have they got to lose? It's not rocket science, and it was most unfortunate for Simon that he was carrying that same item of equipment that had been previously allegedly been lost, and it was most unfortunate that their patrol took that route, and it was most unfortunate that the area had been used so many times before.

A member of a covert operations team who knew Simon was sure that it was that reason why the bomb detonated, as the following day instructions were sent out ordering immediate variations in the use of the same item of electrical equipment. "Over that period those that wore the white sifter including myself were informed to use discretion as to when to turn the white sifter on or off." The same person returned to Northern Ireland the following year and received a lesson during training which taught a different technique in using the same piece of kit compared to that he had used in 1991. He explained his distrust in it and explained his reasons why. The instructor got quite flustered and did not give a reasoned response to his answer. Is this, I wonder, a cover-up for someone's neglect? But, this may have been too late as the horse had already bolted. One similar situation was noticeable after the murder of Lance-Bombadier Stephen Restorick at the permanent vehicle checkpoint at Bessbrook Mill in South Armagh. Very shortly after he was shot, a large cover-from-view screen was erected at the checkpoint so that soldiers were not visible from outside whilst checking vehicles entering the check point.

As a response to the 'many stones unturned' I resorted to writing two detailed letters in the hope that the points could be investigated and the results come out in the open. These two letters took the form of one to the PSNI to clarify several police issues and the second to the MoD to clarify several army issues. The PSNI have a department known as the Serious Crime and Review Team, which is a team of senior officers who, as it states, review serious crimes. They are there to assist relatives who, like me, wanted questions answering. I asked the police to elaborate and comment on the following, and they gave the relevant answers.

I asked if anybody had been arrested or convicted for Simon's murder. I did not ask or expect any names to be mentioned. Their reply was "There is no record in the case papers of any one having been arrested or convicted for Simon's murder". They stated that the case was investigated as fully as possible given the area and prevailing circumstances. All lines of enquiry were pursued and the case remains open should any further enquiries arise. The review team went onto say that although nobody was made responsible for Simon's death, available records indicate that two persons suspected of involvement in Simon's murder were later arrested over serious terrorist crimes in South Armagh. Both refused to speak and were released with no further action taken. During the initial investigation, given the isolated nature of the area i.e. the dense wood and the fact that it was in South Armagh, the police experienced a lack of interest and support from the public in that area. The area was therefore secured for two days to concentrate on the recovery of forensic evidence.

I then asked whether the IED placed in Carrickovaddy Wood had any connection with the body of Thomas Oliver, which was placed a short distance away only 4 weeks before Simon was killed. My thoughts were that given the fact that the IED was concealed and well-placed by the IRA, Thomas Oliver's body was placed so close in the IRA's hope that cordon troops would have used Carrickovaddy Wood. The response from the PSNI was that the case papers did not contain any link between the two. I interviewed a member of Simon's platoon who told me that intelligence information was passed down which detailed the following: "A few facts which made his death even more tragic was that the bomb which killed Simon was intended for a patrol weeks earlier that were providing cover whilst the body of an alleged informer was being recovered. That patrol never entered the forest where the device was planted. And the IRA just never went back to recover the device, which sometimes they did if it contained technology the authorities were unaware of and if they didn't want to risk it being recovered, and falling into the authorities' possession. Instead those responsible warned off the occupants of a house on the perimeter of the forest not to let their children play in the wood."

In relation to the information supplied by the individual from military intelligence that one of the terrorists responsible for the IED in Carrickovaddy Wood was killed in the Army operation in Coalisland, the PSNI showed no connection between the two and was unable to comment on the accuracy of any information supplied by the military source.

I asked the police to comment on the speculation surrounding the loss of electrical equipment and whether it had any involvement in the construction and method of initiation of the device in Carrickovaddy Wood. They replied that their research had failed to uncover a statement from the ATO. They do confirm that a full compliment of electrical protection equipment was carried by the patrol, but found nothing to suggest that the electrical item contributed to the initiation of the device. The review team also liased with the Royal Military Police Special Investigation Branch who found no record of such equipment being lost. That's not to say that it did not happen. The police were unable to comment further on the matter.

I gave the MoD the opportunity to comment on several army issues that I felt I should raise with them. I asked them to comment on the issue of the photographic montage that was lost and I supplied evidence that I had to confirm this. The evidence took the form of comments and confirmation from patrol members, comments made in the national newspaper and those in the book that details the many deaths in Northern Ireland over the years. Their reply was that according to the archive search completed, an incident was located on 15th July 1991 that reports the loss of a montage of photos by a patrol from the Coldstream Guards. However there is no full case file or any record of unit action following the loss. This loss was four days before Thomas Oliver's body was dumped.

I asked for the MoD's comments regarding Carrickovaddy wood itself. I put the evidence to them that similar secluded areas are attractive to patrolling troops for searches and lie-ups. I firmed that up with the comments made on the statement from the patrol commander who stated that he had used the wood only a few weeks before the explosion. The comments made by the company commander on the serious incident report stated that the wood had been used at least three times since March 1991 by the Newtownhamilton Ops Company, and that visiting the same wood on several occasions would have meant that patterns were set and identified by the terrorists. The MOD confirmed that the wood had been searched a number of times in the past 18 months since February 1990. This was as a result of a sighting, by helicopter, of a suspected weapons exchange in February 1990, but there is no evidence to suggest it had been over-patrolled prior to the explosion in which Simon lost his life. They did go onto admit, however, that the army had been patrolling the area for a number of years. In a wide-ranging trawl of the departmental archives they identified in excess of 360 boxes relating to Carrickovaddy Wood during the period between February 1990 and August 1991. They describe a box as that which contains five reams of photocopying paper.

I asked the MoD to comment on the alleged circumstances of the loss of the electrical item of equipment. Some months before the Coldstream Guards deployed to South Armagh it was alleged a soldier from a different regiment misplaced an item of 'sensitive electrical equipment' whilst on patrol which was subsequently lost and never recovered.

There was speculation that the same item had come into the hands of the IRA who, having worked out how it operated, then constructed an explosive device, which would detonate if anybody passed it carrying that same item of equipment. Simon was carrying that item of equipment when he passed the concealed device that detonated at that time. It was the first time in the province that this type of device initiation, known as the Victim-Operated Electronic Switch, had occurred. This information had been confirmed to me by many people, some of whom had worked in the bomb disposal department. So great was the concern following the explosion that very shortly after, the operational procedures for the carriage of such electrical equipment was amended. Being a serving soldier in Northern Ireland I too received such instructions.

What I find also interesting and somewhat concerning is the information I was told when I made enquiries with EOD to view their reports and comments of the explosion so that it would help my research. When I explained to a member of the EOD team the information I would like to review he was happy to help. However, when I re-contacted him some weeks later to obtain the information I was told that I could not view it as it was at a 'secret' level and would remain so until 30 years had elapsed. He told me that it was because the army and MOD were still working on procedures to prevent a reoccurrence. The MOD replied: "In your letter you have speculated on what triggered the explosion, and that lessons have not been learnt. I would like to assure you that this is not the case. The Army continually reviews its procedures in light of all operational incidents and applies the lessons it learns with the aim of taking steps to prevent a reoccurrence. You have also raised some issues in respect of technical countermeasures, but given the sensitive nature of this technology it would be inappropriate to comment."

Simon was the first, and up until the end of Operation Banner in July 2007, remains the only soldier to be killed by this new type of victim-operated improvised explosive device. The IRA is forever developing significant modern tactics and equipment and this was one of them, although two other similar devices were recovered in the same area of South Armagh.

At the beginning of 2006 the Police Service of Northern Ireland set up the Historical Enquiries Team (HET), with its sole aim to reinvestigate and reexamine all deaths attributed to the security situation from 1968–1998. All cases will be assessed, reviewed and reinvestigated by a specially selected team of detectives and administrators. Initially it was expected that it would take six years to reinvestigate all the deaths, but in March 2008, only two years into the enquiry, I received a letter from the HET informing me that they have only just completed investigating up to 1972. It would be a long wait to see if any closure would come for Simon.

I spent just over two and a half years of my career in Northern Ireland – the Army flew me out shortly after my 18th birthday and again two years later they flew me out on my 20th birthday. Though I experienced a desperate loss when the IRA murdered my brother, my period 'across the water' gave me some good times. Northern Ireland is a place of beautiful, tranquil countryside and scenery which for 38 years was marred by terrorism. The fields and streets were bloodied, which had a dramatic effect on people from all walks of life. It is not all that are bad – there are people that supported the army's deployment and many that did not. Many people have lost their lives and many people have lifelong physical and mental scars. But it is peace in our time that has brought an end to wasteful violence. We Will Remember Them, and all those who have to live their lives in constant memory of the conflict.

Related titles published by Helion & Company

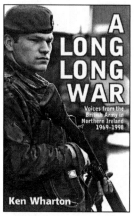

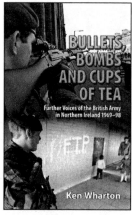

*A Long Long War. Voices from the British
Army in Northern Ireland 1969-98*
Ken Wharton
528pp, photos, maps
Paperback
ISBN 978-1-906033-79-8

*Bullets, Bombs and Cups of Tea.
Further Voices of the British Army
in Northern Ireland 1969-98*
Ken Wharton
544pp, photos, maps
Hardback
ISBN 978-1-906033-34-7

A selection of forthcoming titles

*A Journey to Hell and Back. A Photographic Record of the
Patrols Platoon, 3 Para, in Afghanistan 2006*
J. Scott & D. Edwards   ISBN 978-1-906033-71-2

*Secrets of the Cold War. US Army Europe's Intelligence & Counter-
intelligence activities against the Soviets during the Cold War*
Leland C. McCaslin   ISBN 978-1-906033-91-0

The History of the British Film & Photographic Unit in the Second World War
Dr Fred McGlade   ISBN 978-1-906033-94-1

HELION & COMPANY
26 Willow Road, Solihull, West Midlands B91 1UE, England
Telephone 0121 705 3393   Fax 0121 711 4075
Website: http://www.helion.co.uk